Legends of
GOLF

NEILTAPPIN and PATRICK**MORGAN**

Legends of
GOLF

This revised edition first published in the UK in 2007

© Green Umbrella Publishing 2007

Printed and bound in China

ISBN: 978-1-905828-34-0

CONTENTS

Legends of
GOLF

SEVERIANO**BALLESTEROS** 6–9

PATTY**BERG** 10–11

JAMES**BRAID** 12–15

BILLY**CASPER** 16–17

HENRY**COTTON** 18–19

JOHN**DALY** 20–23

LAURA**DAVIES** 24–27

ROBERTO**DEVICENZO** 28–29

ERNIE**ELS** 30–33

NICK**FALDO** 34–37

RAY**FLOYD** 38–41

WALTER**HAGEN** 42–45

BEN**HOGAN** 46–49

HALE**IRWIN** 50–53

TONY**JACKLIN** 54–57

BOBBY**JONES** 58–61

BERNHARD**LANGER** 62–65

GENE**LITTLER** 66–67

BOBBY**LOCKE** 68–69

NANCY**LOPEZ** 70–71

SANDY**LYLE** 72–73

PHIL**MICKELSON** 74–75

JOHNNY**MILLER** 76–77

COLIN**MONTGOMERIE** 78–81

OLDTOM**MORRIS** 82–83

YOUNGTOM**MORRIS** 84–85

BYRON**NELSON** 86–87

JACK**NICKLAUS** 88–91

GREG**NORMAN** 92–93

JOSÉMARÍA**OLAZÁBAL** 94–97

MARK**O'MEARA** 98–99

ARNOLD**PALMER** 100–103

GARY**PLAYER** 104–107

NICK**PRICE** 108–111

GENE**SARAZEN** 112–115

VIJAY**SINGH** 116–119

SAM**SNEAD** 120–123

ANNIKA**SORENSTAM** 124–125

PAYNE**STEWART** 126–129

CURTIS**STRANGE** 130–131

JH**TAYLOR** 132–135

PETER**THOMPSON** 136–137

LEE**TREVINO** 138–141

HARRY**VARDON** 142–143

TOM**WATSON** 144–147

KATHY**WHITWORTH** 148–149

TIGER**WOODS** 150–153

IAN**WOOSNAM** 154–155

MICKEY**WRIGHT** 156–157

BABE**ZAHARIAS** 158–159

SEVERIANO
BALLESTEROS

Born: Pedrena, Spain April 9, 1957

Turned Professional: 1974

·**Masters:** Winner in 1980, 1983

US Open: 3rd in 1987

Open: Winner in 1979, 1984, 1988

USPGA: 5th in 1984

Ryder Cup record: Member of 8 European teams
(1979, 1983, 1985, 1987, 1989, 1991, 1993, 1995) Played 37,
Won 20, Lost 12, Halved 5. Captain in 1997

When Severiano Ballesteros was at the peak of his powers there was no situation too hopeless that he couldn't muster a miraculous recovery. Whether it was a low punch under a canopy of branches or a raking hook past water or sand, Seve always had the answer. He had the imagination and instinctive natural skill to recover from just about anywhere but it was never as if he had a "laissez-faire" attitude towards the game – he cared deeply about every shot and had a steely determination to match his Spanish flair. Quite simply, Seve had the x-factor, an indescribable character trait that made him the most dashing European golfer of them all.

Severiano Ballesteros was born in Santander in 1957 and grew up within close proximity of the Real Club de Golf de Pedrena. He was the youngest of four brothers all of whom became professional golfers, following in the footsteps of their uncle, Ramon Sota. One of the first Spanish players to make his mark on the world game, Ramon won a handful of professional tournaments and finished sixth in the Masters. His achievements revealed a route into lucrative tournament golf his nephew was desperate to follow.

Seve's instinctive ability to manufacture unlikely shots can be traced back to his early involvement in the game. At the age of seven he had one club – a 3-iron – and would hit shots on the beach or sneak on to the course at dusk to play a few holes. Without strategic or technical guidance he developed a unique eye for the game and learned that even a straight-faced 3-iron could be manipulated to cope with any scenario. Golf quickly became an obsession

for Seve and by the age of 12 he was a scratch player. School simply didn't fit in to his masterplan and by January 1974, Ballesteros had left to become Spain's youngest professional golfer at the age of 16.

By 1976 the Spaniard was beginning to make his mark in Europe. He won his first serious event, the Dutch Open and as leader of the Continental Order of Merit he qualified to play in the Open at Birkdale. But despite having established himself on Tour, he was still relatively unknown and the press had difficulties pronouncing his name. The 19-year-old matched Johnny Miller to share the lead after three rounds. Through the final afternoon, Seve gradually fell away as Miller accelerated but he made a late birdie rush to finish second, tied with Jack Nicklaus. The Open of 1976 offered the public a teaser of what was to come and three years later Ballesteros returned to the Lancashire coast to win his first major.

Heading into the final round at Lytham, Seve was two shots behind the reigning US Open

BELOW
Seve in action at
Wentworth in 1985.

SEVERIANO**BALLESTEROS**

Champion, Hale Irwin. He piled the pressure on his more experienced opponent by making a birdie two at the opening hole and by the time they reached the 3rd tee, Ballesteros was standing proud at the head of the field with a one shot lead. Typically wayward off the tee throughout the round, he constantly offered a chink of light to the chasing pack before slamming the door with an audacious recovery. At the short par-4 16th, he pushed his drive into a television compound, pitched onto the green and holed out for birdie. He took the title by three shots from Jack Nicklaus and Ben Crenshaw and at 22, was the youngest winner of the Open since Young Tom Morris.

When Ballesteros arrived at Augusta for the 1980 Masters he was a major force within the game but American audiences were yet to see the best of him. He laid on a stunning short game display and at one stage during the final round led by a staggering 10 shots. But even at his best Seve was unpredictable and his lead was reduced to two as he stuttered through Amen Corner. He recovered well to win by four and become the first European to win the Masters.

His most memorable triumph however, came at St. Andrews in 1984. Ballesteros was up against two of the leading players of the time – Bernhard Langer and Tom Watson – in a captivating three-way battle (Watson was bidding to equal Harry Vardon's record of six Open victories). Seve showed his class by parring the 17th after finding rough to the left of the fairway. Then, thinking that he needed a birdie on the last, he duly delivered. A two shot victory in spectacular style at the home of golf, confirmed Seve's place among the game's legends.

Alongside his achievements in the Majors, Seve was also a fine matchplay competitor. He played in the Ryder Cup eight times, winning 20 matches and captained the team at Valderrama in Spain in 1997. Ballesteros relished the chance to take on the best players from the States and his genuine passion for the event was crucial in raising its profile to the captivating international event that we love today.

Plagued by persistent back problems throughout his career Seve's recent attempts to compete (albeit sporadically) have proved unsuccessful. But whenever he does play, vast crowds are afforded brief glimpses of the magic that captivated audiences for over two decades. His unique, fearless eye for plotting a successful route to the hole remains one of his most attractive qualities.

Legends of **GOLF**

PATTY**BERG**

It was obvious fairly early on in Patricia Jane Berg's life that here was a young woman who would make a big impact on the world of sport one way or another. Her school days saw the freckle-faced, red-haired Minneapolis tomboy making a mark in speed skating and American football – she played at quarterback on the same 50th Street Tigers team that featured the famed coach Bud Wilkinson – but it was after she first picked up a golf club at the age of 13 that she really came to the world's notice.

She embarked on her career in the Minneapolis City Championship in 1933, and went on to win that tournament the following year. The next milestone was reached when she made the final of the 1935 US Women's Amateur, where she lost to Glenna Collett Vare, and there then followed a truly remarkable life dedicated to golf.

In all, Patty got her hands on 29 amateur and 60 professional titles, including an LPGA record 15 majors, in a career that didn't really end until 1980. And all the time she was visiting golf courses and winning, she was also putting an immense amount of herself back into the game, playing exhibitions and holding instructional clinics for the benefit of golfers less gifted than herself. Patty thought she'd held around 10,000 of these events during her lifetime, and she was always revered for her ambassadorial qualities.

Having already played for the US in the 1936 and 1938 Curtis Cups, she turned professional in 1940 and promptly won the 1941 Western Open. A car crash and World War II interrupted her career but, after serving as a lieutenant in the Marines, she launched herself back into business with a victory in the first US Women's Open in 1946, the only time the tournament was played as matchplay. Thereafter, for a decade, the women's pro game belonged to Patty Berg along with Babe Zacharias.

It was those two, with Louise Suggs and Betty Jameson, who dominated the women's pro game after the formation of the Ladies Professional Golf Association, and in fact Patty was the LPGA's first president from 1950 to 1952. She made her mark on the fledgling tour by winning tournament after tournament, and in fact she racked up 44 wins between the years of 1948 and 1962.

It was in that year that her final victory came, at the Muskogee Civitan Open. By that time, Patty had been the LPGA money leader in 1954, 1955 and 1957 and

Born: Minneapolis, Minnesota, USA
February 13, 1918

Died: September 10, 2006

Turned professional: 1940

US Women's Open: Winner in 1946, 2nd in 1957, 3rd in 1953

LPGA Championship: 2nd in 1956, 1959

Titleholders Championship: Winner in 1937, 1938, 1939, 1948, 1953, 1955, 1957

Western Open: Winner in 1941, 1943, 1948, 1951, 1955, 1957, 1958

Legends of **GOLF**

the game; and was honoured by the LPGA in 1978 when it established the Patty Berg Award in recognition of an outstanding contribution to women's golf. Fittingly, the Patty Berg Award went to the woman after whom it was named in 1990.

She carried on being true to her words, "Don't think that you really win until you live up to that high thing within you that makes you do your best, no matter what," right up until the end. And that end, as a result of Alzheimer's disease at the age of 88, robbed the world of a remarkable woman.

LEFT
Patty Berg in action, watched by a group of spectators.

BELOW
Patty Berg driving during a four-ball foursomes competition at Sandy Lodge Club, 1936.

become the first woman to record a hole in one in a USGA competition when she holed out from the tee at the 1959 US Women's Open at Churchill Valley Country Club in Pittsburgh.

But her career was a long way from being over when she registered that last win in 1962. Patty continued to play despite being plagued by illnesses and injuries throughout her life. Even as late as 1991, when she was 73 and still playing golf for the fun of it, she holed in one. And golf was a lot of fun for Patty Berg. That's one reason why she was so highly regarded by all who practise the game.

Patty stood only 5ht 2ins, yet she could dominate a golf course with astonishing flair, technique, determination and know-how. She was one of the greatest shotmakers the women's game has ever known, a fact acknowledged by fellow professional Carol Mann when she described Patty as "the most knowledgeable person, man or woman, of different golf shots that I've ever known."

The awards and achievements in recognition of her contribution to golf came thick and fast, and they are too numerous to be listed here. Suffice it to say that she was voted the Associated Press Woman Athlete of the Year three times, in 1938, 1942 and 1955; she received the Bob Jones Award, given by the United States Golf Association to recognise outstanding sportsmanship in

JAMES**BRAID**

Born: Earlsferry, Fife, Scotland 1870
Died: November 27, 1950
Turned professional: 1896
Open: Winner in 1901, 1905, 1906, 1908, 1910

Born in Earlsferry in Fife in 1870, James Braid grew up between the two great golfing centres of the time, Mussleburgh and St. Andrews, and through his formative years was a regular on the links at Elie, playing and practising whenever he could. As a teenager, Braid was a joiner by trade but worked hard to flourish on the course and by the age of 16, played to a handicap of scratch.

For James Braid, golf became a profession in 1893 when a friend, CR Smith offered him a job as a clubmaker for the Army and Navy store in London. Despite never having constructed a golf club before, his ability as a craftsman and knowledge of the game served him well. The Scotsman's migration south of the border also created opportunities to compete against some high-calibre opponents. In 1893 he won his first event as a professional, playing alongside his cousin, Douglas Rolland at Limpsfield. The following year he competed in a challenge match at West Drayton against JH Taylor (the reigning Open Champion), squaring the contest on the final hole. These impressive performances confirmed Braid as a player of serious note and his growing reputation allowed him to land the role as professional at Romford Golf Club in 1896 – a job that offered a secure income and an excellent platform from which to develop as a player. Then in 1904 he became the first professional at Walton Heath in Surrey.

Unlike Vardon and Taylor, James Braid had to wait for his graduation to golf's top table. He made his first appearance in the Open at St. George's in 1894 where he finished a creditable 10th and two years later at Muirfield he pocketed five pounds for finishing sixth. Then in 1897 he was runner-up to Harold Hilton at Hoylake. When his time finally arrived in 1901, he went on to win the Open five times in 10 years.

The victory in 1901 at Muirfield was emphatic. Despite shooting 80 in the final round Braid finished three shots ahead of Vardon and four in front of Taylor (the latter was bidding for his third consecutive title). This triumph also served to redress the dramatic shift in the balance of power to English golfers at the Championship. Braid was the first Scottish winner since Willie Auchterlonie, eight years previously.

At 6ft 1ins, James Braid was a tall man with a powerful game, he had a strong grip that delivered a piercing right-to-left ball flight. At his best, his touch on the greens (which became his great weakness later in his career) complimented his powerful long game and Braid achieved back-to-back Open wins in 1905 and 1906 at St. Andrews and Muirfield respectively. His next victory at Prestwick in 1908 was by a staggering eight shot

BELOW
Braid plays out of a bunker.

margin over the Lancashire based golfer, Tom Ball. His fifth and final Open crown arrived at The Home of Golf in 1910 courtesy of a comfortable four shot victory over Sandy Herd. Through his decade of supremacy Braid also won the premier matchplay event that was sponsored by the News of the World on four occasions.

As the Scottish member of 'The Great Triumvirate', James Braid's astonishing list of achievements on the course provide an important chapter in the history of our game. But his lasting legacy is for being an intelligent and prolific golf course architect. His unique signature can be seen on over hundreds of courses, from Troon in Scotland to Ballybunion in Ireland. His style was to use the character of the landscape to provide natural protection and definition. Each layout is distinctive for Braid carried no preconceptions about the type of holes he wanted to build, he simply used the natural lie of the land to determine the character of the course.

The most famous of his designs include the King's and Queen's courses at Gleneagles, Rosemont and Dalmahoy. All have stood the test of time, holding firm in the face of relentless advances in equipment technology, still testing every facet of the game.

James Braid played regularly against members at Walton Heath (he is still remembered at the Surrey club

with great affection) right up until his death in 1950 at the age of 80. In his latter years he would play challenge matches with the aim of beating his age and his competitive drive meant that he often succeeded.

Despite his considerable stature, James Braid was a gentle man with an instinctive game. He had a fierce determination to succeed that enabled him to catch Vardon and JH Taylor whose careers at the top level both started a step ahead. But Braid's accomplishments as a player were equalled by his considerable feats as a golf course architect. Punctuating the British landscape they provide a lasting monument to his influence on the game.

BILLY**CASPER**

There's a commonly held theory in golf that Billy Casper was the most underrated player of all time. Well, he won't be underrated on these pages, for Casper was truly one of the game's greats.

For a measure of the man's abilities, just consider these stats: Billy Casper won 51 times on the PGA Tour, a number surpassed only by Sam Snead, Jack Nicklaus, Ben Hogan, Arnold Palmer, Tiger Woods and Byron Nelson; between 1964 and 1970, he won 27 PGA tournaments – four more than Nicklaus and eight more than Palmer and Gary Player combined, and he won more Ryder Cup points than any other American.

The list of supporting statistics could go on and on but, to get a feel for how good Casper really was, it's also worth listening to the opinions of his fellow professionals. His legendary magical ability with the

putter was summed up by Chi Chi Rodriguez, who remarked: "Billy Casper could make a 40-foot putt just by winking at it."

Listen also to the words of Johnny Miller, who once said: "It's been pointed out that, from 1965 through 1970, the Big Three [Nicklaus, Palmer and Player] combined for a total of 35 victories on the PGA Tour. But Billy Casper won 23 all by himself. That says something about Casper, who in my mind is the most underrated golfer of all time, hands down."

The truth is that, while Casper was notching up all those tournament wins, claiming three victories in the majors and winning the Vardon Trophy (for the lowest scoring average of the year) five times, he was playing in the shadow of the Big Three. If that glamorous and exciting trio had not been around, the quiet and unassuming Casper would doubtless have been feted as the greatest golfer of his era.

The young Billy Casper was introduced to the game by his father at the precocious age of five, and grew up in the same environment, in San Diego, California, that produced other golf legends including Gene Littler and Mickey Wright. He claimed his first win on the PGA Tour – the Labatt Open – in 1956, and it wasn't long before he made his mark on a major championship.

At Winged Foot, New York, in the 1959 US Open, Casper shot 71-68-69-74 for a total of 282, beating off the challenge of Robert R Rosburg by one stroke. He had led all the way from the second round and was undeterred by the thunderstorms that struck the third day and forced the one-day postponement of the final round.

Casper had to wait, perfecting his mesmeric short game and accuracy off the tee, until 1966 for his next major to come along – but what a win it was.

The occasion was the US Open at the Olympic Country Club, San Francisco, and with nine holes to play, Arnold Palmer looked home and dry: Casper was trailing him by seven strokes. But over those final nine

> **Born:** San Diego, California, USA June 24, 1931
> **Turned professional:** 1956
> **Masters:** Winner in 1970, tied 2nd in 1969
> **US Open:** Winner in 1959, 1966
> **USPGA:** 2nd in 1958, 1971, tied 2nd in 1965, tied 3rd in 1966
> **Ryder Cup record:** Member of 8 US teams (1961, 1963, 1965, 1967, 1969, 1971, 1973, 1975). Played 37, Won 20, Lost 10, Halved 7

Legends of **GOLF**

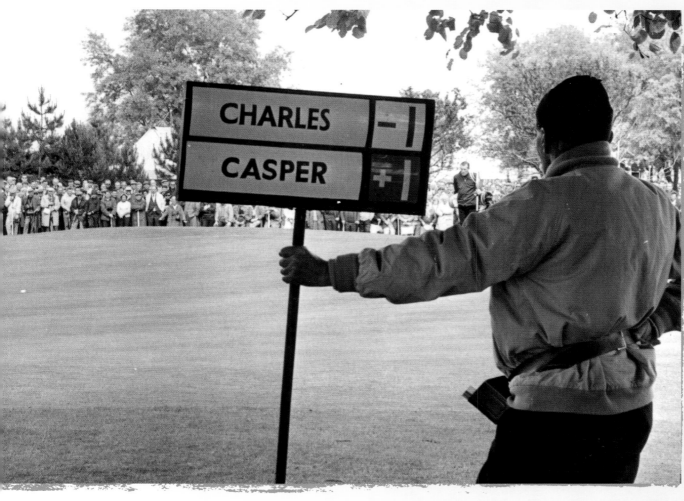

holes, Casper reeled Palmer in bit by bit, scoring 32 to Palmer's 39, recovering five strokes in three holes and taking Arnie to a play-off.

Arnie's army of fans were delighted when the great man streaked into a two-stroke lead on the outward nine holes of the playoff. But they had reckoned without Casper's miraculous putting. Billy sank a 50-foot putt on the 13th to give him a birdie and tie with Palmer, who then watched as Casper calmly built a lead and finished four strokes ahead. One of the greatest US Opens of all time ended in defeat for one of the greatest players of all time.

Casper was not yet finished in the majors, and his next triumph again came via a playoff. This time it was the 1970 Masters, and this time the extra holes saw him up against his old friend Gene Littler.

Billy's winning margin was considerable – five strokes – and yet, typically, he refused to accept much credit, instead praising his caddie, Matthew Palmer, for his role in the victory. "Matthew is responsible for me being here," he told reporters as he tried on the Green Jacket. "He has an exceptional talent for reading the greens."

And that was it as far as majors were concerned, but Casper – who was a major contributor to America's Ryder Cup successes between 1961 and 1975 – was far from finished. When his PGA Tour days were done, he graced the Champions Tour, winning eight times and counting the 1983 US Senior Open among those successes.

It was just a pity he never really received the attention his exceptional ability deserved.

HENRY **COTTON**

If it hadn't been for a typically stubborn dispute with a headmaster, the game of golf might have been denied the enormous contribution of Henry Cotton to its development. The head teacher in question, in charge of the private school Cotton attended, banned the young man from playing cricket, to which the wilful Cotton replied that, in that case, he would play golf from that day on.

That headmaster certainly did golf a massive favour. Cotton went on to become one of the brightest stars in the golf firmament, and his devotion to his art, and to the lot of his fellow professionals, earned him a knighthood in the final days of his life.

Cotton, who ended his career with four PGA Tour titles – including three Open Championships – to his name, as well as 30 victories on the European Tour, was the dominant name in British golf for a long time, even though he was robbed of what might have been his best years by World War II. And his off-course activities did just as much as his shot-making to endear him to the British nation.

First, he worked hard at changing the way his fellow professionals were treated by the, at times, stuffy golf establishment. Pros were often not allowed in the clubhouse at that time, a situation Cotton found intolerable and railed against. And, while the accepted dress code of the time insisted on a jacket and tie, he would sometimes turn up in more casual attire. Henry Cotton was nobody's fool, and no man's servant.

And when his playing career was over, this flamboyant character – who enjoyed a champagne lifestyle and was seldom out of the public eye for very long – continued to serve the game by teaching, writing books and newspaper columns and designing golf courses. He was also instrumental in the founding of the Golf Foundation, giving youngsters a start in the game.

Cotton was a strong man and he was blessed with superb natural technique, but he worked incredibly hard at maintaining it in tip-top condition. He would spend hours in practice, sometimes hitting endless 5-iron shots using just his left arm.

The hard work paid off in spades. He was just 17 when he turned professional in 1924, but he took care to learn more about the game wherever he could, travelling to America to study the greats of the time in action. He started winning tournaments in 1925, but it was the Open Championship of 1934 that really

Born: Holmes Chapel, Cheshire, England
January 26, 1907
Died: December 22, 1987
Turned professional: 1924
Open: Winner 1934, 1937, 1948
Ryder Cup record: Member of 3 Great Britain teams (1929, 1937, 1947).
Played 6, Won 2, Lost 4, Halved 0. Captain in 1947, 1953

LEFT
Henry Cotton competes in the Ryder Cup at the Portland Golf Club, Portland, Oregon, 1947.

BELOW
Cotton demonstrating his swing, 1927.

of his ability to produce the spectacular, and on this occasion he obliged by shooting a course record 66 in the second round on his way to getting his hands on the Claret Jug again.

By now, though, Cotton was 41 and past his peak. He continued to win tournaments as late as 1954, he served as captain of the Great Britain and Ireland Ryder Cup team for the second time in 1953, and his last appearance in the Open came in 1977, but most of the latter part of his life was dedicated to serving golf in an off-course capacity.

"To be a champion, you must act like one," Henry Cotton once said. He certainly always acted the part.

brought him to the world's attention. It wasn't just the manner of Cotton's victory that endeared him to the galleries; it was also the fact that it ended a period of American dominance of the Open that had lasted a decade.

At Royal St George's in Sandwich, Cotton produced opening rounds of 67 and 65 – Dunlop named its best-selling golf ball after that legendary second round – and the opposition was looking routed. The final day dawned with Cotton holding a 10-stroke lead and seemingly strolling to victory. Then nerves struck and his game went to pieces.

Suffering from tension-induced stomach cramps, Cotton struggled round in 79, with the chasing pack reeling in his lead at every hole. But his score was still enough to give him victory by a five-stroke margin.

By the time he won the Open again, in 1937 at Carnoustie, Cotton was on top of the world and in the best form of his life. But he was forced to wait for his third Open title – and perhaps robbed of a few more – by the intervention of World War II. Serving in the Royal Air Force, he nevertheless kept his hand in, organising exhibition matches to raise funds for the Red Cross. His efforts earned him an MBE after the war.

He was not to be denied his third Open Championship, and it duly arrived in 1948, at Muirfield. Cotton was never one to deprive the crowds

JOHN**DALY**

Born: Carmichael, California, USA April 28, 1966

Turned professional: 1987

Masters: Tied 3rd in 1993

US Open: Tied 27th in 1996

Open: Winner in 1995

USPGA: Winner in 1991

When John Daly burst onto the public stage by winning the USPGA Championship in 1991 the golfing world suddenly had a new mega star. But Daly has always been a flawed hero, his game fluctuating between grand success and epic failure. Alcohol and marital problems have lingered throughout his career and it is precisely because he is not the perfect golfing machine that crowds find him such a captivating character.

Born in California in 1966 John Daly soon learnt not to get too attached to one particular area. His father, Jim, worked on nuclear power plants and the family moved home regularly through his early years. From the age of four, when his father handed him two shortened clubs, golf was a crucial part in John's life. Towards the end of his teenage years his interest in other sports, most notably baseball and football, waned and golf started to receive his full attention. He won important amateur championships in Arkansas and Missouri at the age of 18 and these considerable achievements landed him a place at Arkansas University. But for Daly one year in higher education was enough and in 1987, he set about plying his trade as a professional golfer.

His first three years as a tournament player were spent competing on minor tours in America and South Africa. In 1990 he finished ninth on the Hogan Tour moneylist and the self-belief gained from a consistent season provided the launch pad for a successful campaign at PGA Tour qualifying school in 1991.

Daly arrived at Crooked Stick for the USPGA Championship after an unspectacular rookie season

hoping that, as ninth reserve, other players would drop out to allow him a spot in the field. Events conspired in his favour and, despite not having played the course in practice, Daly shot 69 in the opening round. He continued to attack the enormous 7,289 yard layout with typical aggression and rounds of 67, 69 and 71 followed to yield a three shot victory over Bruce Lietzke.

For many, his triumph at Crooked Stick was their first glimpse of John Daly. His long, unrestricted swing appeared to defy the laws of physics let alone those governing a successful technique, and his exciting blend of power and aggression captivated American audiences. His first major success made him an instant celebrity but his new-found fame further unsettled his turbulent private life. Daly's fiery on-off relationship with his wife Bettye Fulford escalated into a fist-fight during a Christmas party in 1992 and he was arrested for third degree assault and suspended from the Tour. Realising that alcohol had played a destructive role in

BELOW
Daly in action at the 1995 USPGA.

this episode he checked into an addiction treatment clinic in Arizona.

Between 1993 and 1995 Daly's private life continued to move at breakneck speed as he divorced Bettye and married Paulette Dean, who was pregnant with his child. By contrast, his on-course development stalled – his most notable achievement during this period being a third place finish in the 1993 Masters. Moving into the 1995 Open at St. Andrews there was little to suggest that Daly could win but the Old Course rewarded his aggression. Typically, JD opted for the driver as many others played for position with irons. His four round total of 282 was equalled by Constantino Rocca who holed a remarkable 70ft putt on the final green to force a play-off. But Daly was unfazed by the Italian's dramatic

LEFT
Daly waves to the crowd on his way to Open victory in 1995.

FAR LEFT
John Daly wins the USPGA in 1991.

finale and dominated the four additional holes, winning by four shots to pocket the £125,000 first place cheque.

John Daly's second Major victory confirmed his status as one of the most naturally gifted players the game has ever seen but his addiction to alcohol remained a destructive and uncontrollable influence. In 1996 he registered just three top 10 finishes and as his game continued to fragment through the following year Paulette filed for divorce. Equipment sponsors came and went as, time after time, Daly proved himself to be a loose cannon – in the 1998 Bay Hill Invitational he recorded a score of 18 on the final hole after hitting six shots into the water.

The first signs of a revival appeared in 2001 when Daly captured the BMW International Open on the European Tour, earning a spot in the world's top 50. In 2004 he won the Buick Invitational and his renaissance continued into 2005. That year saw him reaching playoffs in two tournaments, against the mighty Tiger Woods and Vijay Singh. History records, however, that he lost both, and he made little impact in 2006.

Regardless of whether he is booming 300-yard drives down the middle of the fairway or throwing his putter into a greenside lake, excitement comes guaranteed with John Daly.

His two major victories were triumphs of pure natural talent, red letter days for a man plagued by personal problems. Galleries around the world continue to show their adoration for a flawed hero who has battled hard to conquer his demons.

LAURA**DAVIES**

Born: Coventry, England October 5, 1963

Turned professional: 1985

Kraft Nabisco Championship: 2nd in 1994

LPGA Championship: Winner in 1994, 1996

US Women's Open: Winner in 1987

Du Maurier Classic/Women's British Open: Winner in 1996

Solheim cup record: Member of 9 European teams (1990, 1992, 1994, 1996, 1998, 2000, 2002, 2003, 2005) Played 32, Won 16, Lost 13, Halved 3

Just as Arnold Palmer and Severiano Ballesteros had done for the men's game, so Laura Davies has shown a rare and exciting blend of power and finesse to raise the profile of women's golf. Before her arrival no British player had won major events on US soil but her instinctive game was capable of meeting the challenges of any golf course in the world. By winning national championships in a host of different countries she broke into previously uncharted territory and proved that an English girl could reach the pinnacle of professional golf.

Laura Davies has always had a distinctive look on the course. Her sizeable frame and eye-catching dress sense suit a swing that contradicts many of the basic principles behind a successful technique. Indeed, her unique style can be traced back to her early involvement with the game.

Laura was introduced to golf by her older brother, Tony and would hitch a lift to the local golf club with her mother as she drove to work. Davies remained at the club, playing and practising until her mother returned at the end of the day. Without any professional guidance she developed an unorthodox but instinctive technique capable of generating fast clubhead speed and impressive distance. This was coupled with a naturally deft touch that enabled her to compete throughout her teenage years with great success. Having made an impact with the Surrey county girls team, she went on to win both South East and Intermediate English Championships before playing in the 1984 Curtis Cup.

Her ascent through the amateur ranks had successfully prepared Davies for life on Tour by 1985. But to finance her travels around Europe, she was forced to borrow £1,000 from her mother. The pressure of this financial burden and the desperate desire to prove herself at the top level inspired Davies to a second place finish at the Hennessy Cognac Ladies Cup in Paris just two weeks after setting out on Tour. A cheque for £4,000 allowed Davies to repay her mother's generosity and continue her successful rookie season – she finished 11th in the US Women's Open before winning the same title in Britain.

When she arrived at Plainfield in New Jersey for the US Women's Open of 1987 she was still relatively unknown. But after 72 holes Davies had announced herself to the world, tying JoAnne Carter and Ayako Okamoto for the lead. No British player had ever won the event and up against far more experienced opponents, few expected Davies to prevail in

BELOW
Davies plays in the Women's World Cup at the Gary Player Country Club, South Africa in 2006.

the 18-hole play-off that ensued. But her powerful game intensified the pressure on her opponents and she won with a score of 71. This exciting victory marked a seminal moment in the evolution of the LPGA Tour. Davies had qualified to play in the event through her performances in Europe and was not a member of the US Tour. The LPGA were forced to amend their constitution to grant the winner of the Open automatic membership to the Tour.

Despite her inception to the most lucrative of female Tours in 1987, Davies retained her ambition to compete on different stages around the world throughout her career. In 1988 she finished 15th on the LPGA Tour moneylist and second in Europe as well as winning once in Japan. She always relished the challenge of pitting her wits against a variety of different courses and fields and in

1994 she became the first player to win on five different Tours in the same year. At this time she was the world's number one player and by taking her dynamic game to all corners of the globe was satisfying her responsibility as the most important ambassador for the sport.

Laura Davies reached the peak of her powers between 1994 and 1996. She won 23 times around the world during this period including three major championships. Her fierce battle at the top of the world rankings with Annika Sorenstam captivated audiences and proved that women's golf was capable of producing genuine sporting superstars.

In addition to helping the spread of women's golf, Laura Davies was also an important figure in the growth of the Solheim Cup. The event was first played in 1990 at Lake Nona in Florida and Davies was part of a European team that were soundly thrashed by their American rivals. At this time many feared the gulf between the two sides would render future encounters pointless but in 1992, Europe won at Dalmahoy and Davies collected three points from three matches. Now into her 40s, she remains an ever-present and her talismanic performances have been essential to the continued competitiveness of the Solheim Cup.

Like many of the great golfers featured in this book, Davies has enjoyed a long career at the highest level and it certainly isn't over yet. Not only is she a regular winner but she plays with a dynamic, all-or-nothing style that embraces power and delicacy in equal measures. She paved the way for fellow Europeans to embark on successful international careers and raised the quality of competition for audiences all around the world.

ROBERTO**DEVICENZO**

A fairly modest total of one Open Championship and four other PGA Tour victories, from a career that spanned six decades, would not normally qualify a player for entry in a book about golf legends. Factor in another 230-plus professional tournament wins around the world, however, and you're suddenly talking about a bona fide superstar.

The player we're talking about is Roberto De Vicenzo, and his long career is truly the stuff of legends.

Born: Buenos Aires, Argentina April 14, 1923
Turned professional: 1938
Masters: 2nd in 1968
Open: Winner in 1967, 2nd in 1950, 3rd in 1949, 1956, 1964, tied 3rd in 1948, 1960, 1969
PGA Tour wins: 4

But it is somewhat tragic that a man with so many triumphs to his name is perhaps best known for a moment of disaster.

The moment arrived at the 1968 Masters. The record books show that the Green Jacket that year went to Bob Goalby, but it could – perhaps should – have been De Vicenzo who slipped on the famous garment. He had played a sensational final round, making light of Augusta National's front nine with a score of 31 and finishing with a 65. The score seemed to have set him up for a play-off with Goalby the following day.

But De Vicenzo's playing partner, Tommy Aaron, had marked a four as the Argentinean's score for the 17th, when in fact De Vicenzo had holed out for a birdie three. The latter signed the erroneous scorecard and, of course, the higher score is the one that shows in the history books, and the one that handed victory to Goalby. De Vicenzo then uttered a remark that followed him for the rest of his career and beyond: "What a stupid I am."

He may have been careless on that occasion, but the same could not be said for his golf. He was a great believer in the merits of solid and frequent practice, often hitting 800 or more balls a day as he prepared for tournaments. His technique drew admiration from all who played against him – Gary Player once described him as one of the three or four best strikers of the ball he ever saw. And he would not be hastened into making his shots: "If you hurry, then nothing seems to go right," he famously said.

De Vicenzo's golf career started as a caddie in his native Buenos Aires, and he turned professional at the tender age of 15. Six years later, he racked up the first of his nine Argentine Open victories, and he was on his way to those 230-plus tournament wins.

While he had a natural liking for his home continent of South America, De Vicenzo won tournaments just about everywhere he played. He plied his trade all over the world and could boast open championship wins in – besides Argentina – Belgium, Brazil, Chile, Colombia, France, Germany, Jamaica, Mexico, the Netherlands, Panama, Peru, Spain and Uruguay. He represented Argentina no fewer than 17 times in the World Cup, and

Legends of **GOLF**

Invitational) and 1968 (the Houston Champions International), and they prefigured three wins on the Senior Tour that included the 1980 US Senior Open.

It wasn't long after that De Vicenzo was inducted into the World Golf Hall of Fame, recognising his immense contribution to the game. That contribution didn't just consist of the multitude of tournament victories, more than any other golfer in history: the fact that he was a genuinely nice guy and a fine ambassador for golf also ensured his place in the pantheon of the greats.

his final triumph in the Argentine Open came in 1985, when the man was 62.

There were many other victories, including wins on the Senior Tour, but none of his trophy-grabbing exploits gained as much attention as his solitary major: the Open Championship of 1967. Roberto had a more than decent overall record in the Open Championship, finishing fifth or higher a very creditable nine times. But at the Royal Liverpool course in Hoylake, while Britain was revelling in the endless Summer of Love, it all came together. And it all came together for De Vicenzo at the ripe old age of 44.

Feeding off the support of the British gallery, who had taken to this likeable man as much as fans anywhere, he set out on the final round two shots ahead of playing partner Gary Player and three ahead of Jack Nicklaus. By the time he arrived at the 529-yard 16th, Nicklaus was just two strokes behind, and on a charge. The stage was set for De Vicenzo to play what he later described as the best shot of his life – a 3-wood from 240 yards that ended up just 20 feet from the hole. It was an extraordinary shot and enough to make him the Open's oldest winner.

De Vicenzo, naturally, regards that win as his greatest achievement, but what of his other PGA Tour victories? They came in 1957 (the Colonial National Invitational and the All-American Open), 1966 (the Dallas Open

ERNIE**ELS**

Born: Johannesburg, South Africa October 17, 1969
Turned professional: 1989
Masters: 2nd in 2000 and 2004
US Open: Winner in 1994, 1997
Open: Winner in 2002
USPGA: Tied 3rd in 1995

Watching Ernie Els boom 300-yard drives and produce delicate chips shots without breaking sweat makes our notoriously taxing game appear simple. The 6ft 3ins South African swings with an elegance and poise that defies his physical make-up and his effortless power has earned him the nickname, "The Big Easy". Like the great South African players before him, Ernie Els has been a treasured ambassador for the sport, raising the popularity and profile of the game by competing in all corners of the globe. Despite the supremacy of Tiger Woods, Ernie Els has emerged as a world class performer with three majors and a host of Tour titles to his name.

Throughout his early years, Ernie Els was a keen and talented sportsman playing cricket, tennis and rugby as well as golf. In fact it was only when he reached the age of 14, that Els picked golf over tennis – he was Eastern Transvaal Junior tennis Champion at 13. With his attention undivided he soon collected important junior titles. In 1984 he travelled to San Diego to compete in the boys category (ages 13 to 14) of the Junior World Championship and emerged victorious from a field that included Phil Mickleson. Two years later he won the South African Amateur and this triggered a flood of offers from American Universities but Els chose to complete his education in South Africa and when he reached the age of 19, turned professional in 1989.

Competing on the Southern Africa Tour (now known as the Sunshine Tour), Els made his mark in 1992. In one season he accumulated six victories including the three major South African events – the Open, PGA and Masters. By equalling Gary Player's achievement his early promise was confirmed and Els was ready to tackle the best players in the world.

In 1993 he announced himself to the world by becoming the first player to complete all four British Open rounds in the 60s. This was an astonishing feat on one of the most fearsome tracks on the Open rota, St. George's but it was only good enough for sixth place. This performance provided a teaser for what would unfold the following year at the US Open.

In 1994 the Championship was making its' seventh appearance at Oakmont and with a list of previous winners that includes Nicklaus, Hogan and Miller the USGA were confident that the very best would rise to the top. After four rounds Els was locked at the head of the leaderboard alongside Loren Roberts and Colin Montgomerie. An 18-hole three-way play-off eliminated the Scot but was unable to separate the other

BELOW
Els plays out of a bunker in the 2005 Asian Open.

two. Els outlasted his American opponent finally prevailing on the 20th hole to become a major winner for the first time, aged 24.

As US Open Champion, Els was still developing his game and the confidence gained from winning his first major was the launchpad for further success in the 90s. In 1997 he completed a hat-trick of World Matchplay titles and the following year he claimed his second US Open crown.

Els overtook Tom Lehman with a final round 69 and once again narrowly held off the challenge of Colin Montgomerie. His victory at Congressional was worth far more than the half a million dollar prizefund – it confirmed the South African as the official world number one.

Although he continued to win regularly on various Tours around the world, Ernie Els remained winless in the big four until 2002. This barren spell can be explained in part by the rise to prominence of Tiger Woods. In 2000 the American was in his prime, winning three consecutive majors pushing Els down into second place twice. That year "The Big Easy" also finished second in the Masters behind Vijay Singh and the disappointment of three near misses hit hard – Els remained winless on the PGA Tour the following year.

Ernie Els hit back in 2002 winning six times worldwide including the Open at Muirfield. With nine holes left to play he held a commanding three-stroke lead and appeared in total command of his game. But the Claret Jug was the one trophy he yearned for more

than any other and in his desperation to finish the job, nerves had a detrimental affect on his golf. His commanding lead evaporated leaving him in a four way play-off with Thomas Levet, Stuart Appleby and Steve Elkington. Despite his disappointing finale, Els knew that he was the form runner and made five consecutive pars under intense pressure to earn his third major title the hard way.

Since winning the Open of 2002, Ernie Els has captured his first World Golf Championship and his sixth World Matchplay. He has also finished at the top of the European Tour's order of merit twice. Now aged 37, his immense power and deft touch are allied by a wealth of experience that continues to make him one of the world's most dangerous competitors.

NICK
FALDO

Born: Welwyn Garden City, England July 18, 1957

Turned professional: 1976

Masters: Winner in 1989, 1990, 1996

US Open: 2nd in 1988

Open: Winner in 1987, 1990, 1992

USPGA: Tied 2nd in 1992

Ryder Cup record: Member of 11 European teams (1977, 979, 1981, 1983, 1985, 1987, 1989, 1991, 1993, 1995, 1997). Played 46, Won 23, Lost 19, Halved 4

Two of the game's most exciting commodities, Jack Nicklaus and Augusta National, combined to ignite Nick Faldo's passion for golf in 1971. Aged 13 he watched the Masters unfold on his parents' brand new colour television set and, despite never having played golf before, was suddenly hooked. Faldo showed maturity beyond his years by taking lessons with Ian Connelly, the professional at Welwyn Garden City, and practising tirelessly for months before actually venturing onto the golf course. Without concerning himself with scores or competing under pressure Faldo grooved the fundamental swing mechanics so crucial for a man of his height and build. This hard work soon paid off and within two years Faldo was playing off a handicap of plus one.

During his amateur career Faldo represented England at various levels but his greatest achievement was to win the English Amateur Championship in 1975, aged 18. With this triumph at the top of his CV he turned professional the following year.

A creditable 58th position in his first European Tour Order of Merit was followed by a more consistent 1977 season. That year he finished eighth on the moneylist, playing his way into the Ryder Cup at Royal Lytham.

As a Ryder Cup rookie his mental strength soon became evident as he forged an unbeaten partnership with fellow Englishman Peter Oosterhuis, before beating the reigning Masters and Open champion, Tom Watson, in the final day singles. The European team was soundly beaten but Faldo had announced himself on the world stage.

From here Faldo made a relentless ascent through the world rankings and won the European Tour Order of Merit in 1983. By the end of the following year Faldo had 11 European Tour titles and four Ryder Cup appearances to his name. But Faldo was yet to succeed at the very highest level a fact that really hit home when he was forced to watch two of his greatest rivals, Sandy Lyle and Seve Ballesteros, picking up major honours.

Enter David Leadbetter, a young Zimbabwean-born golf coach who was beginning to make his name on Tour. Leadbetter told Faldo that to win a major he would need a technique strong enough to withstand the most intense pressure. For all of its aesthetic beauty, Leadbetter felt that Faldo's swing was cursed by too many moving parts that when placed under the microscope could throw the whole swing out of kilter. Together, Faldo and Leadbetter spent two years rebuilding his swing, during which time he continued to compete but the calibre of his performances dropped drastically. By the end of 1986 he had lost his US

Tour card and many questioned if the Englishman was a spent force.

These questions were answered emphatically in 1987.

That year the Open took place at Muirfield, one of the most demanding layouts on the tournament rota. When the wind blew during the final afternoon it became a battle of attrition but Faldo made 18 consecutive pars to record a final round 71. A faultless display of clean ball striking and nerveless short game skill reeled in Paul Azinger, who had led going into the last day.

If ever Faldo needed an endorsement of the previous two years hard work, it arrived emphatically that day in July.

From this success came the self-belief that his swing would thrive under pressure and his results continued to improve. He finished second eight times in 1988, including after a play-off with Curtis Strange for the US Open.

Despite tasting defeat, this head-to-head experience proved invaluable as Faldo defeated another American,

Scott Hoch in a play-off for the 1989 Masters. There followed another Green Jacket and a second Open title in 1990 and during this period Faldo was comfortably the world's best player.

Each of the Englishman's major triumphs are memorable for their sheer tenacity but perhaps his most dramatic success came as he won his final Masters in 1996. Greg Norman had been in imperious form and held a six-shot lead going into the final round but the golfing world watched through their fingers as the Australian's confidence shattered and his long game imploded. Given a glimpse of his playing partner's fragility, Faldo typically raised his game and after a final round 67, compared to Norman's 78, won by five shots.

Having been married three times it would be fair to assume that Nick Faldo's relentless pursuit of glory has had a detrimental impact on his private life. But despite lingering turmoil off the course, his determination and focus on it has never wavered. From the very start, his story is one of hard graft and a stern will to succeed, traits that were the hallmarks of his greatest triumphs.

Legends of **GOLF**

RAY**FLOYD**

Born: Fort Bragg, North Carolina, USA
September 4, 1942

Turned professional: 1961

Masters: Winner in 1976, 2nd in 1992, tied 2nd in 1985, 1990

US Open: Winner in 1986

Open: Tied 2nd in 1978, tied 3rd in 1981

USPGA: Winner in 1969, 1982, tied 2nd in 1976

Ryder Cup record: Member of 8 US teams (1969, 1975, 1977, 1981, 1983, 1985, 1991, 1993). Played 31, Won 12, Lost 16, Halved 3. Captain in 1989

As tough as they come and as talented as most – that was Raymond "Ray" Floyd, the North Carolinian who ended his career with four major titles, 18 other PGA Tour wins and 14 Champions Tour victories in his bag.

Floyd was a powerful hitter who combined that strength with a deftness around the greens that had commentators searching for superlatives. His chipping was especially formidable, and he was also renowned for his ability to keep going and get the job done when lesser men were wilting under the pressure.

But he was almost lost to the game of golf. Floyd was a gifted baseball player in his youth, and at the age of 17 was on the point of accepting an offer to pitch for the Cleveland Indians. Luckily, he turned instead to a professional golf career and joined the PGA Tour in 1963. He won on his 11th outing – the St Petersburg Open – and didn't stop winning on the Tour until 1992.

His early days as a golf pro, however, were marked by a distinct lack of commitment to making the most of himself. The young Floyd enjoyed a party as much as anyone, and it was only when he married his inspirational wife Maria in 1973 that he truly settled down and began to reap the real rewards of his talent.

And what a talent it was. Floyd was capable of burning up a golf course when he was in the mood, and he was certainly in the mood during the 1969 US Open at NCR Country Club in Ohio. That weekend will long be remembered as the time when the South African Gary Player withstood a barrage of demonstrations and assaults and Floyd fended off the great player's brave challenge.

At the 16th hole on the final round, the pair stood toe to toe. Floyd holed a 35-footer for a birdie while Player missed his par, and Floyd later commented: "Honest to God, I was trying to two-putt."

A Player birdie at the 17th and a bunkered approach shot by Floyd at the 18th kept the gallery on the edge of their seats, but while Player missed his birdie chance, Floyd got down in two and sealed a one-stroke win.

It was another remarkable performance that clinched the Masters for Floyd in 1976. He equalled Jack Nicklaus's four-round record score of 271, set back in 1965, and the Golden Bear was left saying: "I really am surprised to see my Masters record tied. I thought it would stand for a long time. Ray just had four super rounds this week."

He certainly did. Floyd was eight shots clear as the final round got under way, and he kept it that way to take his second major.

His third was six years away, and it was back at the USPGA that Floyd got it. It was an incredible

BELOW
Floyd in action, 1977.

performance at Southern Hills in Oklahoma, and if anyone wanted evidence of Floyd's legendary powers of concentration, they got it as he played the sixth hole of the final round. A can of Freon exploding in a nearby concession tent shook the ground and caused consternation among the spectators. Unrattled, Floyd almost made a birdie putt.

He was in unstoppable form that week, opening with a record-equalling 63, setting 36-hole and 54-hole records and never once three-putting over the four days. It was somewhat anti-climactic when a double bogey at the last hole took him over Bobby Nichols's 72-hole

He wasn't finished yet. His last PGA Tour win came when he was 49, by which time he was already playing on the Senior PGA Tour, which later became the Champions Tour. And, you guessed it, he became the first man to win on both the Senior and regular PGA Tours in the same year.

Floyd's later career was just as distinguished as his earlier one. Among his 14 Champions Tour wins were four Senior majors, with his last – the Ford Senior Players Championship – coming as late as 2000. Quite a way to wind down a career that nearly didn't happen at all.

LEFT
Ray Floyd lines up his ball to putt during the US Seniors Open at Cherry Hills Golf Course in Englewood, Colorado.

FAR LEFT
Floyd chips out of a bunker at the US Masters, 1986.

BELOW
Ray Floyd with his fellow Ryder Cup team captain Tony Jacklin in 1989.

record, but it didn't really matter. Floyd had led from gun to tape.

His major-winning days were not over. Fast-forward to 1986, to the US Open at Shinnecock Hills, and we find Floyd shooting a final round of 66 to become, at 43, the oldest ever winner of the Championship. In trying weather conditions, he finished on 270, one under par, for the tournament, two strokes ahead of Lanny Wadkins and Chip Beck.

WALTER**HAGEN**

No 1
497 Yds
BOGEY

Born: Rochester, New York, USA December 21, 1892
Died: October 5, 1969
Turned professional: 1901
US Open: Winner in 1914, 1919
Open: Winner in 1922, 1924, 1928, 1929
USPGA: Winner in 1921, 1924, 1925, 1926, 1927
Ryder Cup record: Captained 6 US teams, playing in 5 of those matches (1927, 1929, 1931, 1933, 1935 (1937)). Played 9, Won 7, Lost 1, Halved 1

Golf and fashion have always been uneasy bedfellows. Without team uniforms or the demands of strenuous exercise dictating basic restrictions, golfers have been free to express their personalities through their clothing. But until Walter Hagen arrived in the early 1900s, players tended to be suited and booted in much the same way with a smart, sophisticated look golfers had always dressed conservatively. Hagen was the first man to really stretch these boundaries and with his natural charm coupled with an immense talent on the course he broadened the appeal of the game.

Walter Hagen hailed from a blue collar, working class family from Rochester in New York. Living within easy reach of the local country club, he worked his way up from caddie to club maker to head professional by the age of 19. Through these impressionable years, he was in regular contact with wealthy club members, their lavish lifestyles and elegant attire left an indelible mark on the young man.

His early graduation to head professional paid well – $1200 for eight months of the year as well as $2 per lesson – so during the four winter months, he was free to enter professional events and it was as a player that Hagen found the spotlight he adored. Having performed well in the US Open of 1913 (he finished in a tie for fourth), he started to develop a reputation as a dangerous competitor. In 1914 a member of his Rochester club offered to pay his travel expenses so that he could return to the US Open in Chicago. Hagen rewarded his sponsor's faith by shooting a record low 68 in the opening round. He led the event from start to finish to claim his first major title.

This victory opened the world to Hagen – he was now a man in demand. During the war he travelled across America playing challenge matches and charity events and endorsing products. His relaxed, lively character was attractive to sponsors as in a world torn apart by bloody conflict, he was able to appreciate that golf was essentially a showbusiness.

In 1919 Hagen took a job as head professional at Oakland Hills. Situated in affluent Detroit, it appeared to be the ideal position, offering a comfortable and secure living. But after winning the US Open for the second time that year, Hagen realised that he could make good money as a player without having the restrictive responsibilities of a club pro. He promptly left his post at Oakland Hills to become the first solely playing professional.

When the war in Europe finished, Hagen was ready to expand his horizons and he crossed the Atlantic for the first time on the Mauritania in 1920, as the

BELOW
Hagen plays a shot in front of a small crowd in 1920.

reigning US Open Champion. The British public were keen to see just how good the best from the US would be and his presence at Royal Cinque Ports created an unprecedented level of interest.

By this time Hagen had the means to live the lavish lifestyle he craved and he arrived at Deal on the Kent coast, chauffeur driven in a hired Daimler. The rules of his golf failed to live up to his snappy outfits and he finished 53rd in a field of 54.

Despite this disappointing display, Hagen showed his devotion to the event for many years to come and in 1922 he took the title. In 1924, after arriving late for qualifying and persuading the organisers to let him compete, he won again. This victory marked a seminal moment in the evolution of our treasured Championship.

Until this point, the Open field was dominated by British players. After Hagen's victory in 1924 the top Americans recognised the importance of the Championship and regularly travelled to Britain, strengthening the competition. Thanks to Hagen's influence, the tournament that we hold in such high regard today became truly international.

Walter Hagen's record in the two major Opens drifts into obscurity when compared to his performances in the USPGA. Until 1958, the USPGA was the premier matchplay event in the tournament calendar and Hagen entered six times from 1924 and only lost once in 30 matches.

Walter Hagen's reputation remains as a showman both on

LEFT
Hagen practises his golf swing on top of the Savoy Hotel in London, in a 1922 publicity shot.

FAR LEFT
Walter Hagen, captain for the USA, receives the Ryder Cup in 1937.

the club dictated that players should not enter the clubhouse to change their shoes so Hagen chose to do so in his car which was parked directly outside the front of the clubhouse!

Emerging from his ostentatious changing room, Hagen cut a striking figure in black and white, dressed from head to toe in the finest materials. Unfortunately,

and off the course, he was a notorious ladies man who was married twice and loved a party. He became a true golfing superstar, bringing life and colour to an intrinsically conservative game. Furthermore, he paved the way for the likes of Jimmy Demaret, Payne Stewart and Ian Poulter to express their characters through their eye-catching clothing.

BEN**HOGAN**

Born: Dublin, Texas, USA August 13, 1912

Died: July 25, 1997

Masters: Winner in 1951, 1953,

US Open: Winner in 1948, 1950, 1951, 1953

Open: Winner in 1953

USPGA: Winner in 1946, 1948

Ryder Cup record: Member of 2 US teams (1947, 1951). Played 3, Won 3. Captain in 1947, 1949, 1967

More than any other player featured in this book, Ben Hogan fought adversity to forge a successful career in golf. The tragedy of his father's suicide, the desperate struggle to make ends meet and the car crash that nearly killed him all contributed to the steely character of one of the finest golfers in the history of the sport. At his best Hogan had an unerring accuracy and deadly short-range putting stroke ally to his single-minded determination.

Ben Hogan was born in Dublin, Texas, in 1912. His father was a mechanic by trade but as the Depression hit in the 1920s he found work hard to come by and struggled to earn enough money to support his family. In the face of mounting financial pressure and persistent health worries Hogan's father shot himself – Ben was just nine years old at the time.

Not that he needed to be told but this tragedy underlined the importance of earning a secure living and Hogan's involvement in golf started as a boy, earning cash by caddying for members at the local Glen Garden Club. He would play whenever the opportunity arose and during his teens entered amateur state events whenever possible. Success may have been limited but Hogan's knowledge of the game was improving all the time and he turned professional at the age of 19.

For the next nine years Hogan would pursue his dream of making it on Tour without any notable success. In 1937 he married Valerie Fox and the two travelled the country in the desperate hope that Ben would make a substantial cheque to cover their expenses. The breakthrough finally came in 1940 when the 28-year-old

Hogan took the North and South Open at Pinehurst. The confidence gained from this overdue victory enabled him to sustain a higher level of performance and he captured the US Tour moneylist in 1940, 41 and 42.

But World War II struck just as his career was gathering momentum and Hogan joined the US Army Air Corps where he served for three years. On his return to competition in 1946 Hogan, or "The Hawk" as he had become known, won his first major – the USPGA. This victory was made even sweeter having narrowly missed out in both the Masters and US Open earlier that year.

Despite stepping up to the highest level of international golf Hogan realised that to fulfill his potential he had to rid himself of the destructive hook that remained a part of his armoury. In 1947, he practiced hard to turn his natural ball flight from a draw into a fade. The result was a shorter but far more consistent shot that he could rely on under

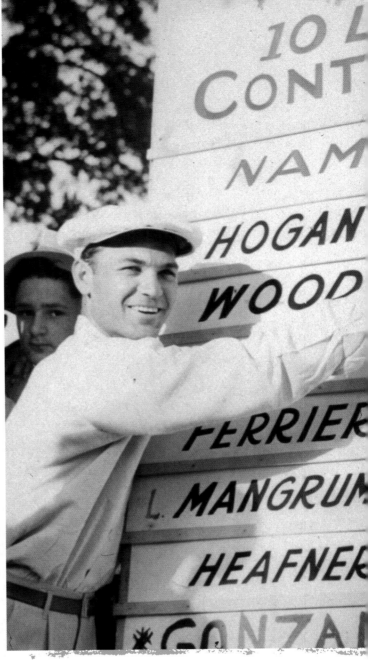

pressure. These changes made him a more potent force and in 1948 he won the US Open and USPGA.

By the start of 1949 Hogan's career was in full swing and he was a serious threat whenever he teed up. But on February 2nd, Hogan was involved in a horrific car crash that left him with numerous broken bones. He spent two months in hospital and did not play golf for the best part of a year.

Walking with a limp Hogan returned to competitive action at the 1950 US Open knowing that 36 holes on the final day might be too much for his weakened by 1953 was yet to enter the Open. But after winning the US Open and Masters that year, he realised that to be remembered as a great champion he needed to complete the British leg of the Grand Slam. He arrived in Scotland to face a brutal 7,200 yard test on a windswept Carnoustie. Showing supreme ball control in difficult conditions, he won by four shots from a group of players that included Peter Thomson.

Hogan was unable to make it back to the States in time for the USPGA but it didn't matter. Aged 40, he had completed the Grand Slam and on his return to New York was given a hero's welcome. His triumph at Carnoustie capped a remarkable year but his major triumphs of 1953 were his last. The yips plagued him for the rest of his career but having triumphed over adversity Hogan had nothing left to prove.

LEFT
Hogan reminds everyone that he has won the Chicago Open in 1941.

FAR LEFT
Hogan on the practise ground.

BELOW
Ben Hogan wins the Open in 1953.

frame. But with typical tenacity he applied himself to the task at hand and managed to force a play-off with George Fazio and Lloyd Mancrum. This meant another round the following day but Hogan mustered the strength for an incredible 69 to take the title. This courageous victory made Ben Hogan the darling of the American public.

Hogan had previously travelled to Britain at the end of 1949 as the non-playing captain of the American Ryder Cup side. It would be fair to say that despite winning the match he did not enjoy the experience and

HALE**IRWIN**

Born: Joplin, Missouri, USA June 3, 1945

Turned professional: 1968

US Open: Winner in 1974, 1979, 1990, tied 3rd in 1975

Open: Tied 2nd in 1983

Ryder Cup record: Member of 5 US teams (1975, 1977, 1979, 1981, 1991). Played 20, Won 13, Lost 5, Halved 2

No follower of golf with access to TV will ever forget the moment in 1991 when Hale Irwin secured the Ryder Cup for the USA. It was the final hole of the final match of the tussle at Kiawah Island between the USA and Europe that became known as The War On The Shore. The supremely talented German Bernhard Langer, up against an Irwin who embodied the Americans' fighting spirit in that contest, needed to sink a six-footer to halve the hole and tie the tournament.

Langer's putt slid just past the cup, and the Ryder Cup returned to the States for the first time in six years. Langer was not the first victim of a golfer with steel in his veins, and he was a long way from being the last. If ever a player was single-minded in his determination to win, that player was Hale Irwin.

You know the saying, 'When the going gets tough, the tough get going'? That sums up Irwin, who sometimes seemed to revel in the most trying conditions a golf course can present. Stories about his attitude to winning are legion, but he probably summed it up best himself: "Take the 20th player on the money list. He may not have won a tournament but he has won a lot of money. He thinks he's a great player. The fans think he's a great player. I don't see it. Don't show me the money; show me what you've won."

Hale Irwin showed an early liking for golf, first picking up a club at the age of four and teaching himself the rudiments of the game on a nine-hole course at Baxter Springs, Kansas. The precocious youngster – also a talented footballer – was

returning sub-70 scores by the time he was 14, and was National Collegiate Athletic Association golf champion in 1967, while he was studying at the University of Colorado.

The prospect of playing golf for a living was appealing, and the young Irwin turned pro in 1968. A wider circle of golf fans could now appreciate the tidiness of his game, the solid excellence of his technique and his burning will to succeed.

Success was not too long in arriving. Irwin's first PGA Tour victory came in the Heritage Classic in 1971, a win he repeated two years later. That tournament was to prove a favourite of his: it was also the last PGA title he ever won, in 1994.

By the time Irwin was ready to take the Champions Tour by storm in 1995 – he has so far amassed a record-breaking 44 wins – he could look back on a tremendously consistent PGA Tour career that featured

20 victories. Most of all, though, he's remembered for his Ryder Cup exploits and his three US Open successes.

And the first of those three wins came in conditions that allowed the never-say-die Irwin to reveal his strength in adversity. Historians believe the 1974 US Open, at Winged Foot in New York State, was played in the most testing conditions imaginable. The fairways were tight, the rough was high and thick and the greens were fast and as hard as concrete.

No player can be said to have conquered Winged Foot on that occasion – indeed the championship was dubbed a massacre – but Irwin toughed it out to win by

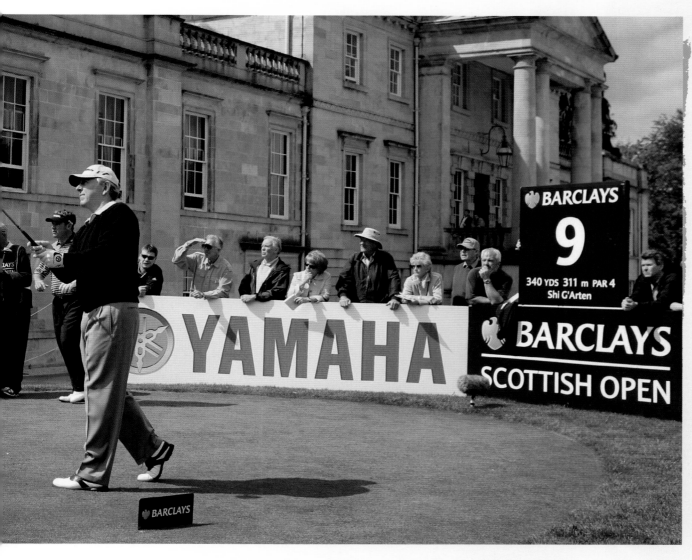

LEFT
Irwin tees off on the
9th hole during the
first round of the
Barclays Scottish
Open at Loch
Lomond, 2006.

FAR LEFT
Hale Irwin on the
putting green, 1985.

two strokes. A glance at his scorecard shows just how testing the course was: he turned in a seven-over-par total of 287.

The second of Irwin's US Open wins came at Inverness, Ohio in 1979. Again, low scores were rare and his final round of 75 was typical of many. But it was enough to ensure he remained at level par for the tournament and defeat Gary Player by two shots.

And at Medinah in 1990, Irwin once again showed his battling qualities to clinch his third US Open win. In the tournament's longest ever play-off, he matched Mike Donald hole for hole before birdieing the 19th in the

sudden-death phase and departing on an uncharacteristically emotional lap of honour of the green.

So at the age of 45, Irwin's reputation as a tough nut to crack was sealed. He could also lay a sound claim to the title Mr Consistency, with his record of making the cut in 86 consecutive tournaments between 1975 and 1978 as evidence.

Then there was his career in the Ryder Cup and his exceptional record of 13 wins from 20 matches. His 4.5 point tally in 1975, from a possible five, put him up there with some of golf's greatest names. Hale Irwin was – still is – a warrior.

TONY**JACKLIN**

Born: Scunthorpe, Lincolnshire, England July 7, 1944
Turned professional: 1962
US Open: Winner in 1970
Open: Winner in 1969, 3rd in 1971, 1972
Ryder Cup record: Member of 7 European teams (1967, 1969, 1971, 1973, 1975, 1977, 1979). Played 35, Won 13, Lost 14, Halved 8. Captain in 1983, 1985, 1987, 1989

British golf fans have a special place in their hearts for Tony Jacklin. This son of a lorry driver almost single-handedly rekindled British interest in the major championships after a long lean spell, then found a new passion, lifting the European Ryder Cup team on to a new plateau of success.

For a brief period, there was no better player of golf on the planet, and his playing days are remembered for the brilliance of his performances in taking the Open Championship in 1969 and the US Open in 1970. The British public took him to their hearts for these wins, and that's not really surprising: he was, after all, the first Englishman to win the Open since 1951, and it had been longer – 50 years, in fact – since a Briton had won the US Open.

Then, when his major-winning days were over, Jacklin, as captain of the continent's Ryder Cup team, piloted Europe to a remarkable upset of the Americans' dominance of the competition.

But Jacklin's career started in modest circumstances. Hailing from the less than glamorous surroundings of the steel-making town of Scunthorpe, he inherited a love of golf from his father and showed great promise as a youngster. He won the Lincolnshire Championship at the age of 13 and thoughts of the professional game were never far from his mind.

As assistant pro at Potters Bar Golf Club in Hertfordshire, long hours of practice honed his game. "As a young man I would practise on my own for hundreds of hours and in my mind Ben Hogan was always standing over my right shoulder making a critique of every shot," he later recalled.

Jacklin was Rookie of the Year on the British circuit in 1962, at the age of 17, and his first professional tournament win came in 1964. Galleries were becoming used to his attacking style and his uncanny accuracy around the greens. TV viewers were treated to a taste of the aggressive Jacklin style in 1967, when his hole in one at the 165-yard 16th at Royal St George's, Sandwich became the first ace televised in Britain.

Victories were by now coming not only in Europe – where he won 22 times during his career – but also in the States. His first PGA Tour win came in 1968, when he claimed the Jacksonville Open, so becoming the first Brit to win a PGA tournament outside of the majors. Greater honours were not long in arriving.

Jacklin's triumph in the 1969 Open Championship at Royal Lytham & St Annes was the first Open win by a Briton since Max Faulkner had got his hands on the Claret Jug in 1951, and it had the effect of inspiring a new generation of British youngsters to take up the game. The following year, the new national hero went one better in becoming the first golfer since Ben Hogan to hold the Open Championship and US Open titles simultaneously, and the first Briton to win the US Open since Ted Ray in 1920.

It was a quite superlative performance at Hazeltine Golf Club. Jacklin simply annihilated a field that included the legendary names of Palmer, Nicklaus and Player, leading from start to finish and winning by a sensational seven-stroke margin. No other player even broke par that week.

But that was the end of Jacklin's major-winning exploits, despite a close call at the 1972 Open when he

Jacklin's enthusiasm and professionalism tore the Cup from American hands for the first time in 28 years, triumphing by 16.5 points to 11.5.

There was even better to come. The USA had never lost in the Ryder Cup on American soil until the occasion in 1987 when Jacklin captained the Europeans to a 15-13 victory at Muirfield Village. Then, two years later, again at The Belfry, he rang down the curtain on his captaincy by steering the team to a 14-14 tie and retention of the trophy.

The passion shown by the European players in those matches set a standard for the years to come, and offered a fitting tribute to a great player.

LEFT
Tony Jacklin escapes from a greenside bunker, 2003.

FAR LEFT
Jacklin in full swing, 1967.

BELOW
Tony Jacklin becomes the first British golfer to win the Open Golf Championship for 18 years, 1969.

was edged out by Lee Trevino. His next major contribution to golf would come in the Ryder Cup.

His Cup playing record was pretty impressive given that it was compiled during a period of American dominance, but things began to change when Jacklin took up the captaincy of the European team in 1983. He, more than anyone, is responsible for the competition becoming the massive media event it is today.

His first inspirational stab at captaincy, at the PGA National Golf Club in Florida, almost saw Europe toppling the USA, missing out by just one point. Two years later, at The Belfry, a European team driven on by

BOBBY**JONES**

Born: Atlanta, Georgia, USA March 17, 1902
Died: December 18, 1971
US Open: Winner in 1923, 1926, 1929, 1930
Open: Winner in 1926, 1927, 1930

When Bobby Jones won the US Amateur Championship of 1930 he became the only golfer in history to capture the national and amateur titles of Britain and America in the same year. "The Impregnable Quadrilateral" as it became known, is a unique achievement that will almost certainly remain untouched. His victories of 1930 were the glorious finale to a seven year period of supremacy in which Jones won seven Opens and six Amateur Championships. But the strain of travelling the world to compete in front of vast, expectant galleries and the stress of living up to his own high expectations pushed him into retirement at the tender age of 28. Thus, memories of Bobby Jones the golfer are of a stylish man in his peak with a smooth swing and a devastating ability to win.

As a child, Bobby Jones suffered perpetual digestive problems and was unable to take solid foods. His ailment forced his parents to move from Atlanta city to the suburbs in the hope that cleaner air would help their son's health. Their new home was within close proximity of the golf club at East Lake and aged five Jones's health steadily improved as he started to play. Like many golfers who begin at an early age, Jones copied the technique of a respected player. Stewart Maiden was the professional at East Lake and without any specific guidance, Jones simply mimicked his swing.

By the age of 13, he had won both junior and senior East Lake club championships and the following year he made his debut in the US Amateur at Merion Cricket Club. The teenager attracted serious media interest as he progressed to the third round of the matchplay phase where he was knocked out by defending champion, Bob Gardner.

Few doubted that Jones was a champion of the future but he was a temperamental young man, prone to throwing clubs and losing his head at the crucial moment. Over the next seven years he would continue to compete in major events without success. In 1921, Jones travelled to Britain to compete in the inaugural Walker Cup matches at Hoylake and after a victorious campaign, he entered the Open at St. Andrews. But after 10 disastrous holes of his third round, he stormed off the course. The 19-year-old was castigated by the press and it was apparent for all to see that his immaturity was costing him dear.

By 1923 Jones had learned to temper his youthful impetuosity and his breakthrough duly arrived at the US Open at Inwood, New York. He had one hand on the trophy with three holes of his final round left

BELOW
Jones tees off, 1921.

to play but finished with two bogeys and a double bogey to fall back into a tie with Bobby Cruickshank. Questions over his mental strength however, were quashed as Jones struck a perfect 4-iron approach to the final green to close out the head-to-head battle with a score of 76 to Cruickshank's 78.

This initial success triggered an avalanche of titles and records over the next seven years. Through this period he won 13 major events and was always either US Open or Amateur champion. He won the British Open three times, his first in 1926 pitted him against Al Waltrous in an exciting final round dual over the links at Hoylake. At the 17th Jones pulled his tee shot into a sandy waste area to the left of the fairway.

Faced with 175 yards to the flag, he fired a fearless long iron approach into the heart of the green. Unnerved by his opponent's miraculous recovery, Waltrous three putted. When Jones went on to win the

US Open that year, he became the first player to capture the two major national championships in the same season.

As Bobby Jones reached his mid-20s, he had just one important title left to win – the British Amateur. The victory he craved arrived in 1930 at St. Andrews. Such was his popularity among the British public, that it is estimated between 12,000 and 15,000 spectators travelled to watch his fourth round match against Cyril Tolley. Jones won an epic encounter on the 19th hole and progressed through five more matches in three days to take the title. He added the Open at Hoylake and US Open at Interlachen to his season's successes before arriving back at Merion for the US Amateur. Victory at the venue of his first ever major appearance would guarantee Jones golfing immortality and he marched mercilessly to the title winning each of his five matches by no worse than 5&4.

While the record books show a man at the top of his profession, dominating fields with apparent ease, the reality was somewhat less glorious. His great friend and journalist OB Keeler always described how Jones suffered terribly with stress during each event. He cared desperately about performing to his absolute optimum and the strain of competing successfully at the highest level for over a decade had taken its toll. In November 1930, Jones announced his retirement.

At the age of 28, Bobby Jones felt that he had achieved all he could as an amateur golfer and embarked on a law career in Atlanta. But there was to be one last chapter in his involvement with the game. Under his supervision, Augusta National was designed by Alister Mackenzie and opened in 1933. The following year the US Masters was born as Jones realised his ambition to establish an invitational strokeplay event between the best players in the world.

BERNHARD**LANGER**

Born: Anhausen, Germany August 27, 1957

Turned professional: 1976

Masters: Winner in 1985, 1993

Open: 2nd in 1981, tied 2nd in 1984, 3rd in 1993, tied 3rd in 1985, 2001

Ryder Cup record: Member of 10 European teams (1981, 1983, 1985, 1987, 1989, 1991, 1993, 1995, 1997, 2002). Played 42, Won 21, Lost 15, Halved 6. Captain in 2004

Before Bernhard Langer came along and charmed the golf world with his determination and skill, Germany wasn't exactly known for its ability to produce world-class golfers. But Langer was responsible for a revolution in the game's popularity in his home country and ensured future generations of Germans would be up there among the best.

Langer was one of the Big Five – along with Seve Ballesteros, Nick Faldo, Sandy Lyle and Ian Woosnam – who put Europe back on the world golf map in the latter part of the 20th century. He made an indelible mark on European golf, won two majors in America and became a firm favourite for his Ryder Cup exploits. And he did all this while battling the 'yips', an affliction that affected his putting game almost from the beginning of his career.

The yips are involuntary motions of the hand or wrist that can ruin the confidence of even the most talented sports performer. When they hit a golfer about to play an important putt, the results can be devastating. But Langer wasn't prepared to be beaten by an affliction that would have sent a lesser man into early retirement, and overcame the problem on numerous occasions, changing grips and putters in his determination to combat the dreaded twitch.

Unlike most German youngsters of the time, Langer felt a huge affinity for golf as a kid, and made up his mind very early that he would earn his living from the game. Wise move. Turning pro in 1976, he was soon winning tournaments in Germany, and his first European Tour win – at the Dunlop Masters – came in 1980. It was the first of 40 victories on the Tour.

But a bigger stage was waiting for this gifted and dedicated golfer. Langer had already made an impact on the Open Championship – finishing second in 1981 – before he conquered Augusta National's fearsome greens to win the 1985 Masters.

At one stage it looked as though Curtis Strange was about to complete one of the greatest comebacks in golf history, after an opening round of 80, but the 27-year-old Langer, in only his second Masters appearance, had the measure of the course. While Strange was struggling to a back-nine 39, he shot a masterful 33 to finish with a 68 and end the tournament six under par.

Eight years later, Augusta again proved a happy hunting ground for Langer, who overcame the course's legendary Amen Corner – the 11th, 12th and 13th holes – on the final round while his rivals fell away.

Langer had registered 10 pars in a row before coming to Amen Corner, and was one stroke ahead of Dan Forsman and two in front of Chip Beck. He parred the 11th and 12th and eagled the 13th, while the best Beck

BELOW
Bernhard Langer (centre) was the European team captain for the Ryder Cup in 2004.

and Forsman could offer were birdies at the 13th. The day ended with Langer at 11 under par for the tournament and four shots ahead of Beck.

America had taken the steady, unassuming Langer to its heart. And American fans had good reason to thank him in 1991, at the infamous "War by the Shore" Ryder Cup. It's ironic that, despite performing valiantly for the European team in 10 Ryder Cups and captaining the team to an astonishing 18.5 – 9.5 victory in 2004, he will perhaps be remembered best in America for a glaring miss that handed the Cup back to the USA.

Ryder Cup, proved an especially tough opponent in foursomes and finished by winning 24 points – more than Ballesteros, for example.

And the culmination of all that good work came at Oakland Hills in 2004, when captain Langer's European troops crushed the USA by the record margin of 18.5 points to 9.5. Every single one of Europe's players paid tribute to the way Langer had organised, inspired, chivvied and supported them from start to finish. His captaincy set a new benchmark for others to match.

LEFT
Langer plays from a bunker at Sawgrass in the USA, 2006.

FAR LEFT
Bernhard Langer celebrates at the 1994 Volvo Masters.

BELOW
Bernhard Langer wins the 1985 US Masters and receives his Green Jacket from Ben Crenshaw the previous year's winner.

It was the last hole of the last singles match at Kiawah Island, in probably the most fiercely contested Ryder Cup there's ever been, and Langer needed to hole a six-footer to halve with Hale Irwin, tie the match and ensure the Cup stayed in European hands. With the golf world holding its breath, Langer's putt slid agonisingly past the hole and Irwin – and the USA, for the first time since 1983 – were the victors.

But that miss really should not be allowed to diminish Langer's simply massive contribution to the European cause. He won half of all his matches in the

GENE**LITTLER**

It's no wonder they called Gene Littler "Gene the Machine". He kept pumping out those shots, year after year, with a fine, consistent swing that drew admiration from all who saw it. Gene Sarazen, no mean striker of a golf ball himself, said it was "a perfect swing, like Sam Snead's – only better".

Littler himself had a simple explanation for the rhythmic beauty of his swing. "I just put ball down and hit," he said.

That witty little description of one of golf's greatest swings was typical of Littler, a man who was known for his dry sense of humour and economy with words. He was also known for the excellence of his golf over a long, long period: the first of his 29 PGA Tour victories came in 1954 and the last arrived in 1977. There was only one year between 1954 and 1979 when he finished outside the top 60 on the money list, and there was a very good reason for that: he had undergone surgery for lymph node cancer. And when his PGA Tour career was finished, he went on to star on the Seniors Tour.

The golf world first began to take notice of Gene Littler in 1953, when he played for the US in the Walker Cup, and followed up that debut by winning the US Amateur Championship. He was still playing as an amateur the following year when he won his first PGA Tour event, the San Diego Open. The year of 1954 provided other milestones for Littler: he turned professional and finished in second place at that year's US Open at Baltusrol.

So began Gene Littler's long pro career and the first couple of years saw him confirming his initial promise. He won four times on the Tour in 1955 and three times in 1956, but the victories started to dry up in 1957, and the well ran dry in 1958. The reason? He had started to tinker with that much-admired swing and his game had suffered. It was time for a consultation with fellow pro and renowned instructor Paul Runyan, and whatever Runyan said, it obviously worked: Littler found himself back in winning ways in 1959, when he claimed five PGA titles. It was his best ever year on the Tour.

Given the seeming ease with which he picked up tournament victories, it's somewhat surprising that Littler only ever won one major championship. That

Born: San Diego, California, USA
November 16, 1930
Turned professional: 1954
Masters: 2nd in 1970
US Open: Winner in 1961, 2nd in 1954
USPGA: 2nd in 1977, tied 3rd in 1966
Ryder Cup record: Member of 7 US teams (1961, 1963, 1965, 1967, 1969, 1971, 1975). Played 27, Won 14, Lost 5, Halved 8

Legends of **GOLF**

LEFT
Gene Littler (3rd from right) poses with the US Ryder Cup team in Scotland, 1965.

victory came in 1961, when he was aged 30 and came out on top of a distinguished field at the Oakland Hills Country Club in Michigan to win the US Open. It was a narrow victory, by a single stroke over Doug Sanders and Bob Goalby, and Littler's performance was remarkable in that he was the only player to break par twice during the championship. In fact, par was only broken 18 times in the entire tournament.

Littler was three shots behind leader Sanders when final-round play commenced, but when it came to the last hole Littler was holding the trump card. Despite taking a bogey five on the 18th, he finished the day with a final-round score of 68, and a total of 281. Sanders needed a birdie at the 72nd hole if he was to tie. His third shot from the edge of the green just missed the cup, and Littler was proclaimed the champ.

Although that US Open victory remained his only major win, Littler came close on several other occasions. The most memorable of those occasions came at the

Masters in 1970, when Billy Casper bettered his childhood friend in a play-off. And it was agonisingly close again in 1977, at the USPGA Championship at Pebble Beach.

Littler had led the field through the first three rounds, but his closing 76 meant Lanny Wadkins was able to secure a tie. The championship went to a sudden-death play-off – for the first time in a major – and Wadkins triumphed at the third hole. So near and yet so far again for Littler.

So it was that he finished his PGA Tour career with just the one major, but Gene Littler wasn't finished yet. His time on the Senior PGA Tour was distinguished, and it got off to a flying start when he won three of the first five tournaments he played. In all, he won eight times on the Senior Tour.

Students of golf should also be impressed by his record in the Ryder Cup. He played seven times for the USA and, from his 27 matches, lost only five times. Gene the Machine just couldn't help winning wherever he went.

BOBBY LOCKE

The first of the great South African golfers, Bobby Locke travelled the world to reach the very top of his profession. Winning important tournaments on three separate continents, his most notable achievement was to triumph in our Open Championship on four occasions. A big man with a rounded swing, Locke hit the ball with a raking draw that verged on a hook and had one of the deadliest putting strokes the game has ever seen. He would navigate his way around the course at his own sedate pace and his unique style, chirpy character and natural talent made him stand out whenever he played.

Born Arthur D'Arcy Locke in 1917 he quickly became known as Bobby for his love of the great Bobby Jones.

Locke's amateur career was brief by comparison to the great American's but provided a glimpse of the glory that was to follow. His first notable triumph came in 1931, at the age of 14, when he won the South African Boys Championship. Then three years later he made his mark on the men's amateur scene by winning the South African Open and Amateur Championships. When he repeated this double in 1937 it confirmed his status as one of the leading amateurs in the game and the following year he graduated to the paid ranks.

As a professional, Locke was quick to announce himself on the world stage, winning the Irish, New Zealand and South African Opens in 1938. But just as his career was blossoming World War II started and Locke joined the South African air force as a bomber pilot, carrying out tours of duty in the western desert and the Mediterranean. On his return to competition in 1946 his two and a half year hiatus from the game did not appear to have hampered his progress as a player as, despite being a few pounds heavier, he won twice in Britain and claimed another South African Open title.

Following the advice of Walter Hagen, Locke then travelled to America in 1947 to become a full time tournament professional. The move brought immediate success as he won four of the first six events that he played in. For three years Locke was a regular on the American circuit, taking at least one title per season and, despite never actually winning, he finished third twice and fourth twice in the US Open. But the story of Bobby Locke's time in the States is not quite as glorious as the records suggest. He was a prolific foreign winner with a deliberate style on the course that made him unpopular with the American crowds (he was often accused of slow play). And when he crossed the Atlantic to compete in Britain in 1949, he was deemed to have broken important contracts and the USGA tried to ban him from entering American tournaments.

Born: Germiston, South Africa November 20, 1917

Turned professional: 1938

Masters: Tied for 13th in 1949

US Open: 3rd in 1947 and 1951

Open: Winner in 1949, 1950, 1952, 1957

Locke's victory in 1957 was his last great triumph as three years later he was involved in a horrific car crash that left him in a coma for several days. He was incredibly fortunate to survive the accident but the permanent damage to his left eye hampered his future performances on the golf course.

His colourful career slowly tailed off but Locke had already reached the pinnacle of his profession, revealing a route to success for the great South African players that followed. His quirky but laid-back character and distinctive style are still fondly remembered, especially in Britain.

LEFT
Locke plays out of a bunker at the 1953 Open, Carnoustie.

BELOW
Bobby Locke with the Open trophy.

This incident encouraged Locke to shift his attention to Europe and in 1949 he won the first of his four Open titles at Sandwich in Kent. After tying with Harry Bradshaw on a four round total of 283, Locke thrashed his accomplished opponent by 12 strokes over a 36-hole play-off.

The following year, he defended his crown on the west coast of Scotland at Royal Troon, beating Roberto Di Vicenzo by two shots. Then in 1952 he defeated his arch rival Peter Thomson by one stroke at Royal Lytham & St. Annes in Lancashire.

However, Locke's final major triumph at St. Andrews in 1957 was marred by controversy. On the 18th green of the final round, Locke moved his marker by the length of his putterhead to clear a route to the hole for his playing partner Bruce Crampton. Locke forgot to return the marker to its original spot and putted out to complete a three-shot victory over Peter Thomson. The incident was later reported to rules officials at the R&A but it was decided that Locke had not received any advantage by moving his ball and was not disqualified. This unfortunate episode understandably rocked the South African so by way of a strange self-punishment he vowed never to play in plus fours again!

During the 50s the intense rivalry between Locke and his Australian counterpart Peter Thomson lit up the game and the pair won eight Open titles in 10 years. But

NANCY**LOPEZ**

What an impact Nancy Lopez made when she first exploded on to the professional scene in 1977 and 1978. Seldom can a player have made such a dramatic entrance.

First, having turned professional in 1977, she finished second in that year's US Women's Open – something she'd already done as an amateur in 1975. Next, in her rookie year of 1978, she rocketed to nationwide fame, clocking up nine LPGA titles – including the LPGA Championship – and along the way claiming five wins in a row.

Her efforts that year won Nancy the Player of the Year and Rookie of the Year titles and earned her the Ladies Professional Golf Association's Vare Trophy, awarded annually to the LPGA golfer with the lowest scoring average. To emphasise the point that she'd arrived in some style, she was also featured on the cover of America's venerable Sports Illustrated magazine.

And to prove that rookie year was no fluke, she went and repeated her success in 1979, walking away with eight more tournament wins. They included the Coca-Cola Classic, in which she triumphed in a sudden-death play-off with Bonnie Bryant.

No one should have been too surprised at the 21-year-old Nancy's success, however, for it had been a long time coming. This smiling young lady who captivated the galleries with her brilliant play and winning personality had been playing golf from the tender age of eight.

The story goes that her father, Domingo, gave Nancy her first set of golf clubs and, when she showed a rare aptitude and love for the game, oversaw her early development. His role is said to have included digging a hole in his back yard and filling it with sand so the young golfer could practise her bunker shots.

Whatever Mr Lopez's methods were, they had the desired effect. By the time she was 12, Nancy had won the New Mexico Women's Amateur tournament and had taken her first steps towards celebrity. She followed up that early success with wins in the 1972 and 1974 US Girls' Junior Championship, and in 1975 entered the US Women's Open as an amateur. As we've seen, she made an immediate impact, finishing in a tie for second place.

And so onward to that astonishing rookie season and the years that followed. Nancy's career record speaks for itself: three major championships, 48 LPGA tour victories, LPGA money leader three times, Vare Trophy winner three times, LPGA Player of the Year four times, member of the 1990 USA Solheim Cup team and team

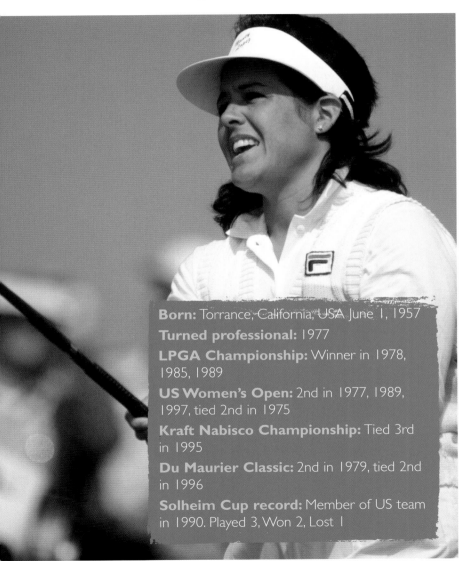

Born: Torrance, California, USA June 1, 1957

Turned professional: 1977

LPGA Championship: Winner in 1978, 1985, 1989

US Women's Open: 2nd in 1977, 1989, 1997, tied 2nd in 1975

Kraft Nabisco Championship: Tied 3rd in 1995

Du Maurier Classic: 2nd in 1979, tied 2nd in 1996

Solheim Cup record: Member of US team in 1990. Played 3, Won 2, Lost 1

Legends of **GOLF**

went one better at 10-under, and Nancy became the first player to record four rounds in the 60s at the Women's Open and not cross the finishing line in first place.

So Nancy was never to win the US Women's Open, despite finishing second four times, and it's surprising that she didn't add more majors to her list of tournament victories. But that doesn't really diminish her overall record, nor the fact that she has made friends wherever she has played.

Perhaps she gained a few of those friends on one of those occasions when she finished second in the Women's Open. It was in 1977, and Nancy is fond of joking about the reason for her failure: her torn trousers in the final round.

LEFT
Respective captains Catrin Nilsmark of Europe and Nancy Lopez of the USA during a press conference for the 2005 Solheim Cup on September 8, 2005.

BELOW
Nancy Lopez prepares to putt, 1995.

captain in 2005 – and all this while she was busy bringing up a family.

Nancy married a fellow athlete, baseball star Ray Knight, in 1982 and a year later gave birth to the first of three daughters. Naturally, bringing up a baby necessitated a break in her golf career, and she played limited seasons in 1983 and 1984. But in 1985, Nancy was back to her full-time winning ways and racked up five tournament wins, five second places and five third places. In addition, she was the leading money earner, took the Vare Trophy and was named LPGA Player of the Year.

Daughter number two arrived in 1986, leading to another short season for this working mother, but there were more victories just around the corner – three times in both 1988 and 1989, for example. Again in 1991, when her third daughter came on the scene, Nancy cut back her tournament appearances, before claiming two more trophies in 1992.

And so it went on, until 1997, when Nancy won her final LPGA tournament: the Chick-fil-A Charity Championship. And that year saw her come as close as she ever did to winning the US Women's Open. It was a remarkable performance, and it would have made a perfect ending to a great career.

Nancy's scorecards at Pumpkin Ridge Golf Club in Oregon read 69-68-69-69, and she finished nine under par for the tournament. Unfortunately, Alison Nicholas

SANDY**LYLE**

In his prime, **Sandy Lyle** was undoubtedly one of the greatest strikers of a golf ball the sport has ever seen. It is therefore rather fitting that the Scot who was born in England will forever be remembered for a perfectly struck 7-iron that crowned him the first British winner of the US Masters.

Lyle had led the 1988 Masters from the first round and at the start of the final day held a two shot lead over Mark Calcavecchia and Ben Crenshaw. But three putts on the treacherous 11th green were followed by a double bogey at 12, where his tee shot found water. Amen Corner looked to have taken another victim as Lyle now trailed Calcavecchia. But the Scot's challenge regained momentum as he made a crucial birdie on the 16th and he reached the final tee needing a par to force a play-off with his American rival.

Having found sand to the left of the 18th fairway with his usually reliable 1-iron, Lyle was faced with 145 yards uphill to a notoriously dangerous green. This was an all-or-nothing moment, a defining passage of play that required total commitment to a technically sound swing. The result was a crisp 7-iron approach that finished around 12ft from the flag, a shot that is now treasured as a glorious part of Augustan folklore. He rolled home the putt and the green jacket was in Scottish hands.

From 1955, Sandy's Glaswegian father, Alex was the head professional at Hawkstone Park and it was in Shropshire that Sandy was born in 1958. Despite growing up around the game, his decision to pursue it seriously came as he watched Tony Jacklin win the 1969 Open at Royal Lytham. Aged 11, Lyle was driven to emulate his hero's spectacular achievement and soon excelled as a talented junior, regularly competing in men's competitions. By the age of 15 his handicap was down to scratch and he was forging an impressive amateur career. When the inevitable opportunity to step up from county to international level arrived in the early 70s, Sandy and Alex had a difficult decision to make. Travelling to and from Scotland would have been both costly and time consuming, so the Lyles decided that Sandy should represent England.

In 1975, at the age of 17, he won international caps at boy's, youth's and senior levels, he also won the English Open Amateur beating Nick Faldo in the process. Two years later, after representing GB&I in the Walker Cup he turned professional, regaining his identity as a true Scot.

For many, life in the professional ranks comes as a shock that requires years of gradual adjustment, but for Lyle the switch brought instant success as he won the qualifying school for the European Tour then

Born: Shrewsbury, England February 9, 1958

Turned professional: 1977

Masters: Winner in 1988

US Open: Tied 16th in 1991

Open: Winner in 1985

USPGA: Tied 16th in 1991

Ryder Cup record: Member of 5 European teams (1979, 1981, 1983, 1985, 1987). Played 18, Won 7, Lost 9, Halved 2

Legends of **GOLF**

followed by two putts and a play-off seemed likely. But the other players failed to capitalise on Lyle's mistake and he became the first British winner of the Open since his hero, Tony Jacklin, 16 years earlier.

The confidence gained from this triumph was the springboard for success in America – he won the Greater Greensboro Open in 1986 and the flagship Tournament Players Championship in 1987. Victory at Augusta in 1988 proved that Lyle had a truly global game that was fit for any course in the world. That year he also won the World Matchplay Championship at Wentworth proving he was also a master of the head-to-head format.

For 30-year-old Sandy Lyle, 1988 was the annus mirabilis that he was never able to recreate. His performances slowly tailed off and top finishes became more and more infrequent. His final European Tour victory came as early as 1992 at the Volvo Masters in Valderrama.

In the years following 1988, Lyle stepped aside to let the likes of Nick Faldo and Seve Ballesteros grab the limelight but the nature of his two major victories still evokes fond memories from those who were desperate to see a breakthrough British success. Furthermore, his triumphs placed European golfers firmly on the international map.

LEFT
Lyle plays out of a bunker at Augusta on his way to winning the Masters.

BELOW
Sandy Lyle receives his Green Jacket from Larry Mize in 1988.

immediately tasted victory at the Nigerian Open. In his first season in the paid ranks he finished 49th on the European Tour Order of Merit, winning the Henry Cotton prize for Rookie of the Year.

During the next decade, Lyle emerged as one of the best players in the world. His consistently high calibre performances, brought a steady flow of titles including the European Open in 1979, the individual World Cup in 1980 (representing Scotland) and the Italian Open in 1984.

By 1985, Lyle seemed destined to claim one of the game's most prestigious prizes for himself. But one month prior to the Open at St. George's, the Scot was hopelessly out of touch. Competing in the Irish Open at Royal Dublin, he needed a par four on the final hole of his opening round to break 90. When he hit his second shot out of bounds, he decided not to return a score. Failure in Ireland inspired Lyle to spend crucial time working on his swing under the tutelage of his father and by mid-July his game was back in shape.

Going into the final round at Royal St. George's, Lyle was sitting three shots behind Bernhard Langer and David Graham. A steady front nine kept him in touch with the leaders and when he made back-to-back birdies at 14 and 15, victory became a real possibility. However, the 468-yard par-4 18th at Sandwich is one of the most demanding finishing holes on the Open rota and when Lyle pulled his second left of the green a poor chip was

PHIL MICKELSON

They often say that, if you want to raise a sporting superstar, you should start 'em young. Usually that means picking up a tennis racquet around the age of eight, or kicking a ball about from four years old. In Phil Mickelson's case, it meant swinging a golf club when he was just 18 months.

Now, at the age of 36, Mickelson shows no sign of tiring of the game after all these years. The year of 2006 saw him putting on the Masters' Green Jacket for the second time, to go with his USPGA Championship win in 2005, and taking his total PGA Tour victories to 29.

If it weren't for the presence on the Tour of a certain Tiger Woods, Mickelson would surely have more trophies in his cabinet. We can be pretty certain there are more to come, though, despite a dismal end to 2006.

Phil Mickelson is an example of a rarity in golf: a world-class left-hander. And most of those in the know would agree that he's the best left-hander the game has ever seen.

He started setting records early on: he became the first left-hander to win the US Amateur title (a distinction that still stands) when he beat the field in 1990. Shortly after, still as an amateur, he won a PGA Tour tournament – the Northern Telecom Open – and his PGA career started to flourish when he turned professional in 1992.

Now big galleries were able to admire his lusty swing and his renowned short game, which helped him to at least one PGA title in each of the years from 1993 to 1998. But there was something missing from Mickelson's curriculum vitae; a glaring omission for such a hugely talented and competitive golfer. That something was a victory in a major tournament.

Mickelson had acquired a reputation as the best golfer never to win a major, and there were some who believed his temperament would always deny him that triumph. A major title was something to which he had come agonisingly close on many occasions, with any number of seconds and thirds in the Masters, the US Open and the USPGA, including three successive runner-up spots in the Masters. Then, in 2004, Mickelson silenced the doubters.

It was the final hole in the final round of the Masters at Augusta National, and Mickelson was faced with a downhill, 18-foot putt for a birdie and victory. He'll

Born: San Diego, California, USA June 16, 1970

Turned professional: 1992

Masters: Winner in 2004, 2006, 3rd in 1996, 2001, 2002, 2003

US Open: 2nd in 1999, 2002, 2004, tied 2nd in 2006

Open: 3rd in 2004

USPGA: Winner in 2005, 2nd in 2001, 3rd in 1994

Ryder Cup record: Member of 6 US teams (1995, 1997, 1999, 2002, 2004, 2006). Played 25, Won 9, Lost 12, Halved 4

Legends of **GOLF**

under par at 281, two strokes ahead of the South African Tim Clark.

On he went to the US Open at Winged Foot, on top of his game and knowing it would take something special to stop him winning. That something special duly turned up, and it wasn't pretty to watch.

At the last hole, Mickelson, having hit his drive way off line, decided to go for the green with his second shot rather than pitch out on to the fairway. Big mistake. He hit a tree, he found a bunker and he ended up with a double bogey, leaving Geoff Ogilvy the rather surprised winner.

OK, there will doubtless be further mistakes as Mickelson's career progresses. There will also be many, many moments to savour.

LEFT
Mickelson hits his tee shot on the 12th hole at the Poipu Bay Golf Course in Kauai, Hawaii, 2004.

BELOW
Phil Mickelson reflects to the media after winning the 2005 PGA Championship.

never do it, grumbled the cynics, he's been in this position before and blown it.

This time he was equal to the task. The difficult putt disappeared underground and Mickelson, at long last, had won a major, finishing with a three-under par 69 and denying Ernie Els by the margin of one stroke. "In the past 10 years, to have come so close and fallen short or having people make critical putts against me, makes this difficult journey towards my first major title so much sweeter," said the jubilant Californian.

Once he'd broken his duck, there was no stopping Mickelson. Next on his major title agenda was the 2005 USPGA Championship at Baltusrol, New Jersey – and in some ways it was a mirror image of the 2004 Masters win. Again, Mickelson needed a birdie at the final hole of the tournament to take the title. And again, he managed it.

This time, though, he was able to showcase his famed "Phil flop" shot when it came to the crunch. Playing out of deep rough, he flopped the ball to within two feet and set up the winning birdie, to the despair of runners-up Thomas Bjorn and Steve Elkington.

It seemed there would be no stopping Mickelson in his quest for majors, and his performance at the 2006 Masters was indeed a dominating one. To take his second Green Jacket in three years, he finished seven

JOHNNY MILLER

There was a time in the mid 1970s when Johnny Miller was just about unbeatable on a golf course. How far his career could have gone if he'd had the unquenchable desire for victory of many of his fellow professionals is anybody's guess.

The blond Californian once compared himself to the great Jack Nicklaus. "When I got to the mountaintop, I kind of looked at the scenery and wondered, 'Now what?' When Jack got there, he said, 'Where's the next mountain?'

It's a crying shame Miller's peak didn't last very long, for when he was on song he was absolutely brilliant,

ranking with the best in the game's history. His masterful strokeplay and pinpoint accuracy dazzled many a gallery from 1973 until 1976, but after that his career declined as his enthusiasm dwindled. So it was that he ended up with no more than 25 PGA Tour victories, including two major championships. It could so easily have been many more.

But let us not dwell too long on the negatives. There is plenty in the Johnny Miller storybook to get golf enthusiasts smiling.

The story started in San Francisco, where young Miller's father encouraged his son's liking for the game. In 1964 he won the US Junior Amateur Championship and, when he was just 19, qualified for the 1966 US Open. In a portent of things to come, he finished a very creditable eighth.

The move to the professional game came in 1969 and Miller started his move to the forefront in 1971, when he won his first PGA Tour event, the Southern Open. Two years later, spectators gazed open-mouthed as he carved out one of the most astonishing rounds of golf ever seen to win the US Open.

As the final round got under way at Oakmont, Pennsylvania, the 26-year-old Miller was six strokes off the lead, which was shared by Julius Boros, Jerry Heard, Arnold Palmer and John Schlee. The unfortunate four – and Tom Weiskopf, who started the day in second position – were quite simply blown off the course as Miller ripped up the US Open record books with a round of 63.

Miller, of course, started his round some little time before the leaders, who must have been thoroughly demoralised as they watched the young man's progress on the leaderboard. Miller's record round contained nine birdies and just the one bogey, and it might have been even lower: his putt at the 18th hit the cup and

Born: San Francisco, California, USA April 29, 1947

Turned professional: 1969

Masters: Tied 2nd in 1971, 1975, 1981

US Open: Winner in 1973

Open: Winner in 1976, tied 2nd in 1973, tied 3rd in 1975

Ryder Cup record: Member of 2 US teams (1975, 1981). Played 6, Won 2, Lost 2, Halved 2

Legends of **GOLF**

tournaments, the last coming as late as 1994, but he never again approached the dizzy heights of his years of glory. His heart just didn't seem to be in it, there were new priorities in his life as his marriage was blessed by the birth of six children and he was, in any case, affected by a series of injuries.

He even decided the Champions Tour wasn't for him, but the world of golf had not heard the last of Johnny Miller. He's now best known as a straight-talking TV broadcaster who is unafraid to express his forthright opinions – opinions that are sometimes less than popular with the players he's describing.

The point is that Miller knows what he's talking about. He's been there, done that.

LEFT
Miller in action at the Open, 1973.

BELOW
Johnny Miller pictured in 1974.

spun out. Even so, he had won his first major by one stroke over Schlee.

So began Miller's purple patch. The year of 1974 saw him win eight PGA tournaments, and he followed up that achievement in 1975 with a further four victories. The following year, he won just the three times – but one of the wins was at the Open Championship.

It's fair to say that Royal Birkdale, the venue for the 1976 Open, was not looking at its best that long, hot summer. The fairways were parched by the fierce heat and lack of rain, and the greens were in poor condition. Not that Miller seemed to mind.

He had moved into second place by the end of a second round in which he scored 68, but the table was headed by a precocious young Spaniard by the name of Seve Ballesteros. The third day – amazingly – saw strong winds and rain, and scores suffered, but Miller and Ballesteros were still fighting it out at the end of the round.

Seve's final round hit big trouble early on, and by the time Miller had played 13 holes, he was eight strokes ahead. He didn't need to birdie the 18th, but that's exactly what he did, and his final round of 66 meant he finished the championship six strokes clear of the rest, and clutching the Claret Jug.

And then… that was pretty much it as far as Miller's career was concerned. OK, he did win further PGA

COLIN
MONTGOMERIE

Born: Glasgow, Scotland July 23, 1963
Turned professional: 1987
Masters: Tied 8th in 1998
US Open: 2nd in 1997, tied 2nd in 2006
Open: 2nd in 2005
USPGA: 2nd in 1995
Ryder Cup record: Member of 8 European teams (1991, 1993, 1995, 1997, 1999, 2002, 2004, 2006) Played 36, Won 20, Lost 9, Halved 7

If performances in the four biggest tournaments were the only true measure of a player's greatness then Colin Montgomerie would not have earned his place in this book of golfing legends. But outside the toughest strokeplay events is a tournament schedule that runs throughout the year, posing unique challenges on a variety of different courses. Competing regularly on Tour requires a level of consistency that success in the majors simply does not, and Colin Montgomerie proved his class by becoming the most prolific money winner in European Tour history. Furthermore, his talismanic performances in eight Ryder Cups have been the single most important factor in the increased potency of the European team.

Born in Glasgow in 1963, Colin Montgomerie is the son of a former secretary at Royal Troon. Growing up on this windy linksland it was inevitable that he and his brother Douglas would develop a healthy passion for the game. Montgomerie was afforded the time to pursue his interest in golf and compete regularly while at Strathallan public school. Having then won a scholarship to Houston Baptist University in Texas his amateur career progressed at a fair pace. He won the 1983 Scottish Youths title and played twice in the Walker Cup before winning the Scottish Amateur Championship in 1987. But despite these considerable achievements it was never Monty's goal to become a professional golfer. Instead, he wanted to use his degree in business management and law to forge a career in golf away from the course. But after graduating from university Montgomerie decided to give life on Tour a try and he turned pro in 1987.

In his first season on the European Tour, Monty revealed his aptitude for team golf, playing for Scotland in the Alfred Dunhill Cup and World Cup. It was an impressive debut season in which he amassed almost £40,000 to become the European Tour's rookie of the year. His maiden victory arrived the following season at the Portuguese Open.

Throughout the 90s Monty was a prolific winner on the European Tour. His unerring accuracy off the tee and precise distance control enabled him to compete on any golf course on the continent. He won tournaments in Sweden, Holland, France and Spain as well as in Britain and captured an astonishing seven consecutive Order of Merit titles. Returning year after year

BELOW
Montgomerie plays in the 2005 Hong Kong Open.

with the determination to maintain his stranglehold over European fields, Montgomerie became the most successful player in the history of the European Tour.

And yet despite consistently proving that he is a world class performer Montgomerie has never been able to make his mark in the majors. With its demands on accuracy and crisp ball striking the Scot has always had the right game for the US Open. At Oakmont in 1994 Montgomerie found himself in a play-off with Ernie Els and Loren Roberts but a round of 78 left him four shots adrift and he was forced to settle back into a tie for second. He also finished second in 1997, just one shot behind the same South African winner. At the 1995 USPGA Steve Elkington sunk a 25ft putt on the first play-off hole to crush his hopes again. It would appear

LEFT
Montgomerie on
the 6th tee at
St. Andrews, 2005.

FAR LEFT
Colin Montgomerie
celebrates victory
over the USA in the
Ryder Cup, 2004.

that the burden carried by the memory of these near misses, coupled with the pressure of meeting his major expectations, has made capturing one of the big four a hurdle the Scotsman simply cannot jump.

Colin Montgomerie's failure to capture any of the big four is a glaring omission on his vast list of achievements, especially when you consider his record in the Ryder Cup. The Scot has played every year since 1991, never losing a singles match and his career total of 23.5 points makes him one of the most successful Ryder Cup players of all time. His most impressive performance was at Oakland Hills in 2004 when after a turbulent year off the course, in which he divorced his wife Eimear, Monty had failed to qualify outright for the team and required a captain's pick from Bernhard

Langer. The 41-year-old Scot repaid his friend's faith by prevailing in three of his four matches and it was fitting that Montgomerie should sink the winning putt as Europe romped to an 18.5 to 9.5 victory.

His role in the triumph at Oakland Hills was the springboard for even greater success in 2005. A second place finish in the Open and victory at the Dunhill Cup (both at the home of golf) returned Montgomerie to the top of the European Tour Order of Merit. That he should scale these heights at the age of 42, having already achieved this milestone seven times previously, is a testament to his determination. But despite his regular victories on Tour and his heroic performances in the Ryder Cup, Montgomerie will not rest easy until he fulfills his potential by winning one of the four biggest prizes.

Legends of **GOLF**

OLDTOM**MORRIS**

In an age when a player's true class is measured by the number of majors he wins and the money he pockets through a seasonal schedule that spans the breadth of the globe, it is hard to quantify the achievements of Old Tom Morris. When he was born in 1821 golf was very much a pastime for the privileged minority, with no professionals or major tournaments. Morris was the first man to make a living as a club pro and he was a regular competitor in the embryonic stages of the Open Championship. Today he is fondly remembered as the founding father of professional golfers.

Born: St. Andrews, Scotland June 16, 1821
Died: May 24, 1908
Turned professional: 1851
Open: Winner in 1861, 1862, 1864, 1867

Old Tom's initial association with the game can be traced back to his job as apprentice to the St. Andrews club, and ball maker Alan Robertson. A skilled craftsman, Robertson was also one of the most accomplished players of the time – in 1858 he became the first man to break 80 at St. Andrews, a record that stood for 30 years. Through the influence of Robertson, Morris developed not only as a craftsman but also as a player.

During the 1840s the pair regularly competed together, forming a formidable foursomes partnership, and in 1849 they played a famous challenge match against the Dunn twins from Musselburgh. Battle took place over three courses – Musselburgh, North Berwick and St. Andrews – with the winning team pocketing a healthy £400. Both sides won on their home courses meaning honours were even heading into the final, neutral venue at North Berwick. Morris and Robertson were four down with eight holes to play but showed typical determination to fight back and remarkably they closed out the match on the final green.

But, sadly, after almost a decade together their relationship ended on a sour note. Robertson had resisted the trend towards manufacturing more durable, gutty golf balls in favour of the age-old, handmade feathery versions. So strongly did he resent the impact of the new ball (it offered greater distance and a smoother roll on the greens) that when Old Tom played in a match using a gutty Robertson was outraged. The two men fell out spectacularly and their differences remained forever irreconcilable.

In 1851 Old Tom moved from St. Andrews to Prestwick, accepting a job as 'custodian of the links'. His role involved all the responsibilities expected of a modern day club professional, with the added obligation of grooming the 12-hole course – all for 15 shillings per week. This meant

Legends of **GOLF**

he was able to continue making clubs and balls, as well as playing regularly with members.

And it was on the links at Prestwick that the Open Championship was born in 1860. With a field of just eight competitors, the first Open was a modest affair that was squeezed into the autumn schedule at Prestwick – to the frustration of many of the members. Morris was one of the game's leading players with an intimate knowledge of the Prestwick layout but the inaugural Championship was won by his great rival from Musselburgh, Willie Park. However, twelve months later Old Tom captured his first Open victory, winning the 1861 event with a 36-hole total of 163 – 11 shots better than Park's score the previous year.

Morris was an ever present at the Open until 1896 winning the title on four occasions through the 1860s. Later, he continued to support the Championship through its evolution from a small event played over 36 holes to the four-round format with scores of strong competitors, played on a cluster of great courses. The exciting international event that we love today evolved through the ardent support of its first competitors – men such as Old Tom Morris.

After 14 years working at Prestwick Morris eventually returned to St. Andrews in 1865. As well as fulfilling his role as custodian of the links Old Tom also turned his

hand to course design and his unique touch can be seen on layouts such as Carnoustie, Lahinch, Royal Dornoch, Nairn and Royal County Down. By adding new courses to the British landscape he helped the game become more accessible and his vision for a links challenge doubtless influenced the great course designers that followed him.

By the time Old Tom Morris died in 1908 golf had grown into a popular sport for the masses. The Open Championship was established as the flagship event, each year crowning another genuine superstar. The influence of Old Tom through the early evolution of the game was invaluable. His role as the first club professional, his support of the Open Championship and his golf course architecture have left a lasting legacy, a crucial chapter in the history of the game.

YOUNGTOM**MORRIS**

Through the 1860s and 70s, Young Tom Morris was golf's star attraction, a young prodigy who seemed more at home on the course than anyone before him, including his father. He was the outstanding talent of his time and despite dying at the tender age of 24, became a crucial figure in the evolution of the Open Championship.

When Young Tom Morris was born in St. Andrews in 1851 golf was an emerging game played by a handful of people on a handful of courses. But for Young Tom, growing up near the 12-hole links at Prestwick under the guidance of his father – the game's first professional, golf was in his blood.

Young Tom quickly developed a sound technique ally to his natural mental fortitude and by the age of 13 was already emerging as a player of serious note. In 1864, he played a challenge match in Perth against a talented local by the name of William Greig. A sizeable crowd turned out to watch Young Tom defeat his skillful opponent.

This performance confirmed that, even as a boy, he was one of the best players in the country and just three years later in 1867 he made his Open debut. His father may have taken the title that year – his fourth and final victory – but Young Tom finished a highly commendable fourth. This early experience proved invaluable and Young Tom returned the following year to make his mark.

Still in its infancy, the Open was played each year at Prestwick attracting small fields of around 15 players that consisted of professionals and various capable members of established golf clubs. The man with the lowest score after three 12-hole rounds was crowned champion and received an ostentatious red leather Moroccan belt that that was decorated with silver buckles.

In 1868, Young Tom Morris triumphed over 12 of the best players of the day (including his father) – it was a victory that marked the beginning of his reign. Aged just 17 at the time, he remains the youngest player ever to have won the Open, a record that looks set to last forever.

The following year pitted the two Morrises against each other in a final round duel as the rest of the field lagged helplessly behind (Bob Kirk finished third, some 11 strokes shy of the winning total). Neither player could claim the advantage of knowing more about the intricacies of the course and it was Young Tom who prevailed by three shots.

By this time, Young Tom Morris was at the height of his powers (he had a hole-in-one on the eighth hole of his opening round) and many other competitors believed that he was simply unbeatable. He duly completed a hat-trick of victories in 1870, defeating his great friend Davie

Born: St. Andrews, Scotland 1851
Died: December 25th, 1875
Open: Winner in 1868, 1869, 1870, 1872

Legends of **GOLF**

sail for St. Andrews but the news on their arrival was not good – both wife and child were dead.

This tragedy clearly rocked Young Tom and returning to St. Andrews to live with his parents, he played very little golf for the remainder of the year. Many believe that his death on Christmas Day in 1895 was the result of a broken heart despite the more scientific medical opinion that cited pneumonia.

By 1872 Young Tom Morris was golf's first real superstar. His impeccable ball striking was matched by a deadly putting stroke – an exciting formula that provoked a new level of interest in the game. And were it not for his hat-trick of victories from 1868 to 1870, the famous Claret Jug may never have been born!

LEFT
The Open Golf Championship entrants for 1865, featuring Young Tom Morris (2nd from top left) and to the immediate right Old Tom Morris.

BELOW
Father and son. Young Tom pictured with his dad Old Tom.

Strath by 12 shots. His winning total of 149 was a record for the three round format that remained unbeaten (the Open became 72 holes in 1891).

The tournament organisers had previously decreed that if a player won the event three times, he was entitled to keep the prize. Young Tom accepted the Moroccan belt and without a trophy to fight for the following year, there was no championship.

In 1872 the members at Prestwick decided that for the Championship to continue it needed additional support from the R&A and the Honourable Company of Edinburgh Golfers. Between them they would pick up the bill for a new trophy. Sadly for Young Tom, who won the Open for the fourth time that year, no trophy had yet been commissioned.

So the iconic image that represents our great championship – the Claret Jug – was born in 1873 when the Open moved from Prestwick for the first time and headed for St. Andrews. But just as Young Tom Morris appeared to be invincible, destined to make the Claret Jug his own, his reign came to an end. His triumph of 1872 was his last – the following three Opens were won by Tom Kidd and Willie and Mungo Park.

In 1875 Young Tom played a challenge match with his father against Willie and Mungo Park at Musselburgh. As he walked off the final green he was handed a telegram explaining that his wife was experiencing complications during the birth of their first child. Young Tom and his father immediately set

BYRON**NELSON**

In 1945, Byron Nelson set a staggering record by winning 11 consecutive tournaments. In one single year his achievements, including 19 tournament victories at a stroke average of 68.83, reveal a gifted man at the very peak of his powers and it was a brief period of total domination that no other player has come close to matching. But there was one crucial component missing from Nelson's psychological make-up – he lacked the same determination that drove other great players to compete year after year and exceed his record of five major victories.

His gruelling 1945 tournament schedule took its toll on Nelson and at the end of the season he retired, aged 34.

Byron Nelson grew up within close proximity of the golf course at the Glen Garden Club in Texas and by the age of 10, he was already earning a wage as a caddie. An ideal occupation for an energetic young boy, Nelson was joined in the caddie ranks at Glen Garden by none other than Ben Hogan. Through their early years the two formed a healthy and friendly rivalry on the course that helped them both develop as strong competitors, sustaining their interest in the game. Throughout the 1930s and 40s Nelson's career progressed ahead of Hogan's and after victory in the 1930 South West Amateur Championship had confirmed that a career in golf could be lucrative, Nelson graduated to the professional ranks in 1932.

His debut season on Tour however, was a bitter disappointment. The success he craved never materialised and for a brief period Nelson sought an alternative career away from the golf course, in the oil business. But when the dust settled on his frustrating start as a tournament golfer, he devoted himself to the game. In 1934 some respectable finishes boosted his finances and enabled him to secure a job as an assistant professional at the Ridgewood Club in New Jersey. Nelson's breakthrough year on Tour came in 1936 – he finished ninth on the moneylist and captured his first significant title, the Metropolitan Open.

Byron Nelson won the first of his five major titles in 1937 at the age of 26. With seven holes left to play at Augusta, he was trailing Ralph Guldahl by four shots. But the infamous risk and reward back nine provided a stunning twist, starting at the par-3 12th. As Nelson birdied, Guldahl found water to score a double bogey five. Sensing that his more experienced opponent was feeling the heat, Nelson bravely attacked the par-5 13th, hitting the green in two. He duly converted his eagle putt and as Guldahl registered a bogey six, Nelson was suddenly

Born: Waxahachie, Texas, USA February 4, 1912
Turned professional: 1932
Masters: Winner in 1937, 1942
US Open: Winner in 1939
Open: 5th in 1937
USPGA: Winner in 1940, 1945
Ryder Cup record: Member of 2 US teams (1937, 1947). Played 4, Won 3, Lost 1. Captain in 1965

Legends of **GOLF**

from haemophilia and was exempt from fighting in the armed forces. Sadly for Nelson, his most spectacular run of form coincided with the closing stages of World War II and with some big names missing, his numerous, emphatic victories were somewhat devalued. In 1945, his aggregate tournament score was an incredible 113 under par, he won $66,000 and his average winning margin was over six shots. His 19 tournament victories included a second USPGA Championship at Dayton, Ohio.

For Nelson, this incredible year brought him all the success he desired. Having journeyed across the length and breadth of America, he was exhausted and with his trophy cabinet bulging, he decided to retire the following year.

Byron Nelson's achievements will forever assure him of a place among the game's elite. The fact that he retired at the age of 34, just as most golfers are reaching their prime, leaves a question mark over just what he might have accomplished had he the natural drive of a Nick Faldo or a Jack Nicklaus.

LEFT
Byron Nelson – honorary starter, plays from the 1st tee on the opening day of the Masters, 1994.

BELOW
Nelson competing in the 1937 Ryder Cup at Royal Birkdale.

sitting proud at the head of the field. He clung on to the lead to take the title with a four round total of 283.

Further US Tour victories followed in 1938 but Nelson was ill at ease with his own game. He believed that to build on this early success his rather loose technique needed tightening. So he set about remodelling his swing and he did not have to wait long for this important decision to be vindicated. He won his only US Open title in 1939, at the expense of one of his great rivals, Sam Snead. Standing on the final tee, Snead needed a par five to take the title but his golf disintegrated and he closed with a devastating eight. This left Nelson, Craig Wood and Denny Shute to fight for the honours in extra time. After 18 holes, Nelson and Wood were tied on 69 with Shute eliminated after a score of 76. Another 18 holes were needed to separate Nelson from Wood, 70 to 73.

Byron Nelson was adept at imposing his will on his opponents as his record in the USPGA reveals. He reached five finals in six years, winning twice during this period. His mental strength was also crucial in capturing the 1942 US Masters. After four rounds, Hogan and Nelson were locked on a total of 280. In an exciting play-off, the two laid on a shotmaking masterclass, with Nelson pipping his great rival by one shot after a sparkling 69.

Between 1939 and 1945, many of the world's top golfers including Sam Snead and Ben Hogan were involved in military service. Nelson however, suffered

JACK
NICKLAUS

Born: Columbus, Ohio, USA January 21, 1940

Turned professional: 1962

Masters: Winner in 1963, 1965, 1966, 1972, 1975, 1986

US Open: Winner in 1962, 1967, 1972, 1980

Open: Winner in 1966, 1970, 1978

USPGA: Winner in 1963, 1971, 1973, 1975, 1980

Ryder Cup record: Member of 6 US teams (1969, 1971, 1973, 1975, 1977, 1981). Played 28, Won 17, Lost 8, Halved 3. Captain in 1983 and 1987

The problem with any discussion about the greatest golfers of all time is that it is impossible to compare players of different generations. Debating whether Hogan would have beaten Ballesteros, or if Jones was a more talented ball striker than Woods is interesting, but ultimately futile. The only quantifiable measure of a golfer's ability lies in his list of achievements, and this is where Jack Nicklaus stands proudly above the rest. For some, crossing the winning line requires the wrestling of mental demons but for Nicklaus it was a natural progression. Quite simply, he was an instinctive winner whose 18 major victories have become the yardstick by which greatness is now measured.

It was evident from an early age that Jack Nicklaus had a special talent for the game. Having been introduced to golf by his father at the age of 10 young Nicklaus was recording scores in the 70s just two years later. He quickly grasped many of the key fundamentals under the tutelage of Jack Grout, the professional at Scioto Country Club in Ohio. Importantly, Grout never tempered the hard-hitting instincts of his star pupil and even as a teenager Nicklaus was notorious for his powerful game. By the age of 16 he was winning state amateur titles and was good enough to earn a place in the field for the US Amateur. He was a crucial member of the winning American Walker Cup team in 1959 and the following year finished second in the US Open, two shots behind Arnold Palmer. It was clear that Nicklaus was a major champion in the making and after winning his second US Amateur title in 1961, he turned pro.

The foundation laid by a relatively long and successful amateur career paid off during his first year in the paid ranks as he won the US Open at Oakmont. At this time Arnold Palmer was the best player in the world and the crowd adored his dynamic gameplan and easy-going character. Conversely, Nicklaus seemed to have a cocky, bullish character to match his stocky physique. When the two men went head-to-head in a play-off for the 1962 US Open it was clear who the public were rooting for. But Nicklaus confirmed his hype, beating his esteemed opponent by three shots.

Nicklaus remained an unpopular winner for some time but as he matured into his late 20s he suddenly relaxed his public persona. He lost weight, grew his hair and started wearing more fashionable clothes – changes that did not go unnoticed by the public – and his popularity grew quickly.

Through the 60s and 70s Nicklaus consistently challenged for and won major honours. When he captured the 1966 Open at Muirfield, he became only the fourth man to complete a Grand Slam – he was just 26 years old. But it wasn't until the 70s that "The Golden Bear" reached his peak, winning seven majors between 1970 and 1975. His career at the highest level continued well into the next decade too, his fifth and final Green Jacket arriving in 1986. Despite experiencing a few relatively barren years on Tour the 46-year-old was still a threat when the biggest prizes were on offer. By making one of his trademark final round charges he accelerated past Greg Norman and Tom Kite to win by a single shot.

In a career filled with so many magnificent successes it might seem strange to focus on his failures but they provide an interesting insight into the character of Jack

By the end of his career, Jack Nicklaus had completed the Grand Slam three times over. There were also countless near misses as the likes of Player, Trevino and Watson held his predictably fierce challenges at bay. Since retiring from the Tour Nicklaus has become a leading figure in golf course architecture. Highly regarded layouts such as Muirfield Village, Castle Pines and Valhalla bear his vision of long carries, well-positioned bunkers and vastly undulating greens. But regardless of his considerable achievements off the course Jack Nicklaus will forever be remembered for a breathtaking game that simply bore no sign of weakness.

LEFT
The Swilcan Bridge, at St. Andrews where Jack made an emotional farewell to the Open.

FAR LEFT
Jack Nicklaus with the Open trophy in 1978, St. Andrews.

BELOW
Nicklaus wins the Masters at aged 46 in 1986.

Nicklaus. After losing an epic battle with Tom Watson in the sunshine at Turnberry during the 1977 Open Nicklaus walked off the final green with his arm around his opponent, offering his congratulations. In the Ryder Cup of 1969 he conceded a short but missable putt on the final green of his crucial singles match against Tony Jacklin (despite having lost to the same man in the morning matches). Nicklaus did not want to see his great rival hand America the Cup by missing from close range. The match was shared and so was the Ryder Cup, ending a decade of US domination in the event. Not even Jack Nicklaus could win them all but it became clear that he was just as gracious in defeat as he was in victory.

GREG**NORMAN**

He's a big man with a big golf game to match, and he's notched up some big achievements over the years. But Greg Norman has probably lost count of the times he came close to adding to his haul of titles only to have victory snatched out of his grasp at the last moment.

Consider these rather distressing facts: "The Great White Shark", as he's known, is one of only two men who have lost all four of the major championships in play-offs; and there was a year, 1986, when his name was at the top of the leaderboard as all four majors entered the final round, yet he claimed victory in only one of them.

Still, there have been plenty of successes to counter the disappointments in the Australian's exciting career. Norman was the dominant figure in the game during a long period of the 1980s and 1990s, and by the time he qualified for the Champions Tour in 2005, he had 20 PGA Tour titles (including two majors), 17 European Tour wins and many, many other victories to his name. For a very long time in the early 1990s – 331 weeks, to be precise – he just could not be dislodged from the top spot in the world rankings.

Yet Norman's aggressive, long-hitting game, distinctive blond hair and flashing smile – no wonder he acquired "The Great White Shark" nickname – were a long time arriving. Unlike many of the players featured in this book, he was not too devoted to golf until his mid-teens, preferring to use his impressive physique to good effect in rugby and Australian Rules football. When he was 15, though, he picked up a taste for golf after caddying for his mother.

His progress was rapid and he turned professional in 1976. Soon, he was earning a respectable living on the European Tour – where his first win came in 1977, at the Martini International – as well as continuing to play, and pick up trophies regularly, in Australia.

By 1982, Norman had become the European Tour's top money winner, and the following year he joined the PGA Tour. Success was not long in arriving as he chalked up victories in the Kemper Open and Canadian Open in 1984. Two years later, he was holding the Claret Jug as Open Champion.

There weren't too many low scores in the first two rounds at Turnberry that year, but Norman's amazing second-round total of 63 – equalling the lowest score ever in the Open Championship – showed that the

Born: Mount Isa, Queensland, Australia February 10, 1955

Turned professional: 1976

Masters: 2nd in 1996, tied 2nd in 1986, 1987, 3rd in 1999, tied 3rd in 1989, 1995

US Open: 2nd in 1984, 1995

Open: Winner in 1986, 1993, tied 2nd in 1989

USPGA: 2nd in 1986, 1993

Faldo. Nick shot a 67 to finish on 269, but Norman was inspired that day. His round score of 64 – it could have been 63 if he hadn't missed a 14-inch putt at the 17th – was described as "awesome" by Gene Sarazen and gave him his second Open by a two-stroke margin.

"I didn't want the round to end," said Norman afterwards. "I wished it could have been 36 holes."

Most golf fans wish Norman's winning PGA career had gone on longer, too. But, after winning his last titles in 1997, he nowadays concentrates on his booming business empire and plays the occasional tournament in Australia. The Great White Shark has claimed his last major victim.

LEFT
Norman at the 1986 US Masters.

BELOW
Greg Norman on the 9th tee at Turnberry in the Open 1986.

course could be conquered. If he hadn't bogeyed the last, he would have stood alone as the sole holder of the low-score record. A dismal third day saw Norman's tournament lead cut to one stroke, but he was back on form for the final round. A score of 69 gave him a total of 280 and a five-stroke victory over the nearest challenger, Gordon J Brand.

If only the rest of 1986 had gone as well for Norman as the Open. As we've seen, he led going into the final round of the other three major championships, only to taste bitter defeat in the Masters and the US Open. And he must have found the last day of the PGA especially hard to take. After looking odds-on to take the Championship, he lost out after going round in 76 and watching Bob Tway hole a miraculous bunker shot.

The near misses continued in 1987, when Norman saw the Masters title slip from his grasp as Larry Mize holed out with an astonishing 45-yard chip. And golf folk still shake their heads sadly at the one Norman threw away in the 1996 Masters, when a last-day 78 and Nick Faldo's round of 67 saw his six-stroke lead turned into a crushing five-stroke victory for the Englishman.

The two men had crossed swords in the final round of a major before. But in the 1993 Open Championship at Royal St George's, everything had gone right for Norman, who started the final round a stroke behind

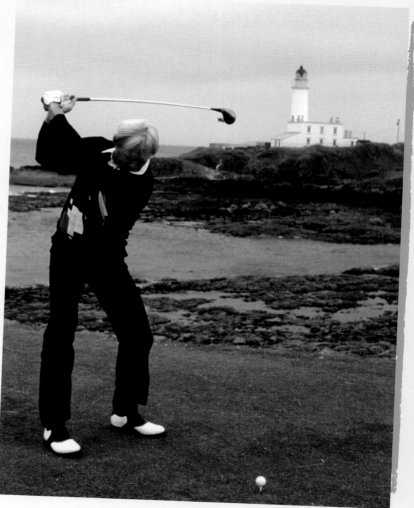

JOSE**MARIAOLAZABAL**

Born: Fuenterrabia, Spain February 5, 1966

Turned professional: 1985

Masters: Winner in 1994, 1999

US Open: Tied 8th in 1990 and 1991

Open: 3rd in 1992

USPGA: Tied 4th in 2000

Ryder Cup record: Member of 6 European teams
(1987, 1989, 1991, 1993, 1997, 1999). Played 28, Won 15,
Lost 8, Halved 5

The career of José María Olazábal was divided into two distinct phases by a mysterious foot injury that threatened to leave him unable to walk. During an 18-month hiatus from competitive action his world ranking plummeted from ninth to 225th. But Olazábal's game was built on a natural aptitude for clean ball striking and a deft touch around the greens, so when he returned to fitness in 1997 few doubted that he was capable of scaling previous heights. With two majors, 25 Tour titles and six Ryder Cup appearances to his name, José María Olazábal has been one of the world's most dangerous competitors for the last two decades.

The Olazábal family home is situated within 100 yards of the 9th green at the Real San Sebastian Golf Club in Northern Spain. Both his father and grandfather worked for a modest wage as greenkeepers, enabling José María to pick up the game at an early age. But unlike fellow Spaniard, Seve Ballesteros who had graduated from caddie to professional by the age of 16 Olazábal was able to develop his game through a long and successful amateur career. In 1983 he captured both Italian and Spanish Amateur Championships as well as the British Boys title. Then in 1984, at the age of 18 he defeated Colin Montgomerie in the final of the British Amateur by 5&4 at Formby. After winning the British Youths title the following year he decided to turn professional and immediately qualified to play on the European Tour.

Being one of the least experienced members on Tour did not phase José María as he was accustomed to success. In his debut season he notched victories at the European Masters and Sanyo Open to finish second on the order of merit. Between 1986 and 1994, Olazábal won 15 times on the European Tour and twice in America. He was emerging as a top class player desperately looking for his first major title.

The course at Augusta National could have been designed with José María's game in mind. Wide fairways flanked by minimal amounts of rough forgive the odd errant tee shot while slick, undulating greens push short game skills to the limit. Throughout his career Olazábal has struggled to tame his driver but from the fairway his approach play remains deadly and his short game is always one of the best on Tour. Having come close to winning the Green Jacket in 1991, when Ian Woosnam pipped him by a single stroke, it was clear that the Masters represented his best chance of breaking into the major winner's circle. He duly did so in 1994 after an epic battle with American, Tom Lehman. The title was decided on the par-5 15th when Olazábal holed a 30ft eagle putt from the fringe. Lehman was closer to

JOSÉMARÍA**OLAZÁBAL**

the hole than his challenger in two but missed his eagle putt and the 28-year-old Spaniard coasted to a two shot victory. Then in 1999 he continued a rich vein of European success in the Masters by holding off a stiff challenge from Greg Norman and Davis Love to win by two once again.

José María Olazábal won the 1994 Masters despite feeling a niggling pain in his feet. As he played through the remainder of the season the problem got progressively worse until he could barely walk. At the end of the year, medical advice cited rheumatoid arthritis but the diagnosis was wrong and the subsequent operation failed to rectify the problem. Unable to walk, let alone play golf during 1996,

Legends of **GOLF**

on American soil in 1987 – they won three of four matches together. In total the Spaniards played in four Ryder Cups, and their partnership yielded a mighty 12 points. They added flair to the European team and injected some genuine passion into the event.

When José María Olazábal reached his peak in the 1990s, he was a regular winner with a fast, compact swing and an unerring putting stroke. His two Green Jackets are a monument to his innate ability to raise his game under intense pressure. Now aged 41, he remains one of the most dangerous and popular European competitors on Tour.

Olazábal sought an alternative opinion and finally, a German doctor discovered that he was suffering from a spinal hernia. Olazábal battled back to fitness through a rigorous and painful regime that combined exercise with physiotherapy. He returned to the European Tour in time for the 1997 Dubai Desert Classic and two weeks later completed a sensational comeback by winning the Turespana Masters Open de Canaria.

The injury to his feet forced him to pull out of the 1995 Ryder Cup at Oak Hill, but the Spaniard has still amassed six appearances in his career to date, winning 17.5 points. His formidable partnership with Seve Ballesteros was crucial in the first ever European victory

MARK O'MEARA

If popularity won major golf tournaments, Mark O'Meara would have ended up with more than just the two to his name. He would also have won them a whole lot earlier.

One of the best-liked players ever to grace the game, O'Meara kept the world waiting a long, long time – until after his 40th birthday, in fact – before he won the major he deserved. And, for the legions of Mark O'Meara fans, it turned out to be just like waiting for a bus: no sooner did one major win arrive than another turned up just behind it.

The records show that O'Meara won his first PGA tournament, the Greater Milwaukee Open, in 1984. Victory after victory followed, in the USA and elsewhere, but it wasn't until 1998 that he registered his first win in a major. It came in April of that year at Augusta National, where O'Meara won the Masters after 14 unsuccessful attempts, and the victory came in some style.

The 41-year-old birdied holes 17 and 18 of the championship's final round to claim a memorable one-hole victory over the likes of Fred Couples and David Duval, becoming as he did so only the third player to birdie the last two holes and win the Masters. The win had other distinctions, too: the fact that O'Meara won at his 15th attempt was a Masters first, and he was only the fifth player in the tournament's history to win after not leading in the first three rounds.

So Mark O'Meara was a happy man before he even landed on British soil in July to take part in the Open Championship at Royal Birkdale. British fans were looking forward to watching the sensation of the era, Tiger Woods, justify his world number one ranking, but it was Tiger's close friend, O'Meara, who came out on top.

In an Open remembered as much for the appallingly wet and windy weather conditions in which much of it was played as for the quality of the golf, O'Meara finished the third day just two shots behind leader Brian Watts and tied with Jesper Parnevik and Jim Furyk.

Battle between Watts and O'Meara was joined on the closing holes of the final day, and the end of the round saw the two tied on 280. In the resultant four-hole play-off, an early O'Meara birdie proved decisive and the man went on to complete a remarkable major double. He had become the oldest player to win two majors in the same year.

Born: Goldsboro, North Carolina, USA
January 13, 1957
Turned professional: 1980
Masters: Winner 1998
US Open: Tied 3rd in 1988
Open: Winner in 1998. Tied 3rd in 1985, 1991
Ryder Cup record: Member of 5 US teams (1985, 1989, 1991, 1997, 1999). Played 14, Won 4, Lost 9, Halved 1

Legends of **GOLF**

and clocked up tournament victories in Japan, France and Argentina among other places.

Meanwhile, he was also busy representing the US in many team competitions, furthering his reputation as a good team player in five Ryder Cups and seven Dunhill Cups. But his form began to slip away after his annus mirabilis of 1998, as a series of injuries took its toll.

It was not until 2004, when O'Meara travelled to Dubai for the Desert Classic and finished ahead of Paul McGinley to claim the prize money, that he registered another official win. It was a victory that effectively rang down the curtain on a career that had included 16 PGA Tour wins and made him a multitude of friends.

To emphasise that 1998 really was the Year of Mark O'Meara, he then went on to beat Tiger and win the Cisco World Match Play Championship, and no one was surprised when he was named PGA Player of the Year.

Modest and self-effacing to the last, O'Meara played down his achievements. "I'm a very nice player, a good player, but I don't classify myself as a great player," he told reporters after his Open triumph. "I consider myself a consistent player who tries to do the best I can at all times. I try to treat my fellow competitors with the utmost respect. Maybe because of that, good things happen."

Good things had been happening to O'Meara since he was 13. It was at that age that his family moved close to a golf course in California, and he and the game started to get on like a house on fire. He won the US Amateur Championship in 1979, turned professional in 1980 and was Rookie of the Year on the PGA Tour the following year. Then, in 1984, came that first PGA Tour win.

While he was waiting for his first major victory to turn up, O'Meara gained a reputation as one of golf's most pleasant personalities, and it was a worldwide reputation. To the pleasure of galleries far and wide, he ventured outside the USA more than most American golfers, to Europe, Australasia, Asia and South America,

ARNOLD**PALMER**

Born: Latrobe, Pennsylvania, USA September 10, 1929

Turned professional: 1954

Masters: Winner in 1958, 1960, 1962, 1964

US Open: Winner in 1960

Open: Winner in 1961, 1962

USPGA: Winner in 1962, 1972

Ryder Cup record: Member of 6 US teams (1961, 1963, 1965, 1967, 1971, 1973). Played 32, Won 22, Lost 8, Halved 2. Captain in 1963 and 1975

Golf's graduation from a minority sport to a global game in which those at the pinnacle can expect to become multi-millionaires was given a mighty push by the swashbuckling Arnold Palmer. His gung-ho gameplan, immense skill and friendly demeanour were all captured on television and he became the all American hero who did more to popularise the sport than any other player on this list. Such was the impact of the "The King" on the golfing world that playing into his 70s he still attracted enormous crowds desperate to pay their respects.

Much like Young Tom Morris over 75 years before Arnold Palmer grew up with golf in his blood. His father, Deacon, left his job as a steel miner in Pennsylvania to become a golf professional at a small local club, ensuring that his young son would have a firm foothold within the game. But unlike Jack Nicklaus and Gary Player, Palmer's progression into professionalism was far from smooth. Despite being the top-ranked player at Wake Forest College Palmer spent three years in the US coastguards and even tried his hand as a salesman before winning the US Amateur in 1954 and settling on a future in golf.

When Palmer did finally emerge as a serious competitor Ben Hogan was the fading super power in the American game. His major victories of 1953 were to be his last and nobody had captured the public's imagination in quite the same way until Palmer swept to victory in the 1958 Masters.

Typically, he left his final round charge to the very last minute, making birdies at the last two holes to pip Doug Ford and Jack Hawkins.

Then in 1960, after winning his second Masters title, Palmer faced a seven shot deficit heading into the final round of the US Open at Cherry Hills in Denver. More importantly there were also 12 highly talented players between himself and leader, Mike Souchak. The tempo for the day was set early on as Palmer made four birdies on the first four holes and reached the turn in just 30 blows.

The cavalier style of this triumph (including an eagle on the 13th) endeared him to the press and public and he went on to appear on the front cover of Sports Illustrated 12 times, as well as becoming one of the few sportsmen to make it onto the front cover of Time magazine.

But it wasn't just in the States that Palmer was capturing the public's imagination. He won our Open Championship twice and in 1961, at Royal Birkdale, he laid on a particularly virtuoso display. With strong winds buffeting the Lancashire coastline only the purest ball strikers were able to compete

BELOW
Palmer at the 1994 US Open plays out the infamous 'church pews' bunker, Oakmont.

Legends of **GOLF**

ARNOLD**PALMER**

and Palmer won the event by a single shot from Dai Rees. Despite the strength of the wind Palmer's strategy was typically bullish. On the par-5 15th during the final round he forced his second shot from deep rough onto the green, a shot that very few others would have even considered. His victory broke the Thomson/Locke era of domination, re-awakening a strong American challenge and adding some much-needed impetus to the Championship. The British public recognised the importance of Palmer's sudden impact and he remains a popular figure on this side of the Atlantic.

On the course, Arnold Palmer lived life on the brink but having such a bold gameplan is a double-edged from deep rough (the triumphant memories of Royal Birkdale were clearly still fresh in his mind). He lost the subsequent play-off by four shots and never did manage to add to his major tally of eight.

Arnold Palmer enriched the game with moments of genuine theatre that unfolded in front of television cameras to growing audiences. He had a common touch and fallibility that brought him closer to the people who paid to watch him play. These qualities meant that when he won it seemed heroic and when he lost, everyone shared in his despair.

LEFT
Palmer in Ryder Cup action, 1973.

FAR LEFT
Palmer at Royal Birkdale in 1961, where he won his first Open title.

BELOW
Arnold Palmer stands next to a plaque unveiled in his honour at the 1995 Masters.

sword and his defeats were often just as spectacular as his victories. Only three months before his triumph at Birkdale Palmer walked up the final fairway at Augusta needing a par-4 to win the Masters. He caught the bunker to the right of the green, thinned his next shot over the other side of the putting surface and then chipped and two putted for a double bogey six. Palmer had handed Gary Player his first Green Jacket on a plate. Then at Olympic Fields, during the US Open of 1966, Palmer threw away a six-shot lead over Billy Casper. He appeared in total control heading into the final few holes but recorded a disastrous run of figures that included a six on the 16th, where he tried to hit a 3-iron

GARY**PLAYER**

Born: Johannesburg, South Africa November 1, 1935
Turned professional: 1953
Masters: Winner in 1961, 1974, 1978
US Open: Winner in 1965
Open: Winner in 1959, 1968, 1974
USPGA: Winner in 1962, 1972

Self-belief is a powerful asset and Gary Player was a master of positive thinking. Without considering anything but the perfect outcome he imposed his will on the course and his opponent. By also working tirelessly on his game and maintaining his peak physical condition Player enjoyed four decades at the highest level. And in the style of all the great South African golfers he travelled extensively, confident that his game would prevail on any course in the world.

Born in Johannesburg in 1935 Gary Player was just six years old when his mother died of cancer. Despite his tender years this tragedy left an indelible mark on the young man as his father, a worker in a gold mine, was left to care and provide for the family. It was Player's father who introduced Gary to the game at the age of 15, and he soon became hooked.

Virginia Park in Johannesburg was the venue for his initial golfing education and under the guidance of the head professional Jock Vewery, Player soon developed a respectable game. Even as a teenager, he had the dedication and discipline to work hard and this maturity enabled him to secure a job as Vewery's assistant before graduating to head professional at Killarney Golf Club. Both placements offered a secure living in Johannesburg albeit without the buzz of competitive golf. Player realised that to fulfil his ambition of golfing for a living he needed to leave South Africa. So aged 19, and without any serious success behind him, Player travelled to Britain to pursue his career as a tournament professional.

At first, Player struggled as tournament golf exposed his developing game and many of his fellow competitors felt that his grip was too strong and his backswing too flat. They made it known that he didn't have the mechanics to compete and advised him to return to his comfortable life as a teaching pro in South Africa. Unperturbed, Player continued to graft as hard as ever and in 1956 he won an important Dunlop sponsored event at Sunningdale.

The following year he crossed the Atlantic to pit his game against the likes of Arnold Palmer and Billy Casper on the US Tour. In 1958 he won the Kentucky Open, adding his name to a rare list of internationals to triumph on American soil. Player was gaining recognition as a serious force and his first major victory arrived at Muirfield in 1959. Aged just 22, he became the second South African to win the Open Championship.

BELOW
Gary Player, on his knees, splashes out of a bunker at the Senior British Open in 1994.

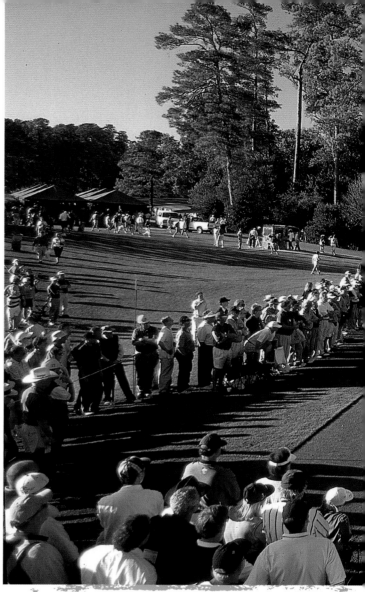

Victories in the Masters (1961) and the USPGA (1962) quickly followed, leaving the US Open as the missing leg of the Grand Slam. But in 1965 he became the third golfer in history to have won all four majors after winning a tight play-off with Kel Nagle. In an extraordinary act of generosity, he donated his $26,000 winner's cheque to the USGA for investment in a cancer charity and junior golf.

Gary Player was a gritty competitor and throughout his career he excelled in the head-to-head format, winning the World Matchplay Championship five times. In 1967 he won an incredible match against Tony Lema despite facing a seven hole deficit at the half way stage. Then on his way to claiming the 1968 title he met Tony Jacklin in the semi-final. Player missed a short putt on the 36th hole to win the match and certain members of the partisan

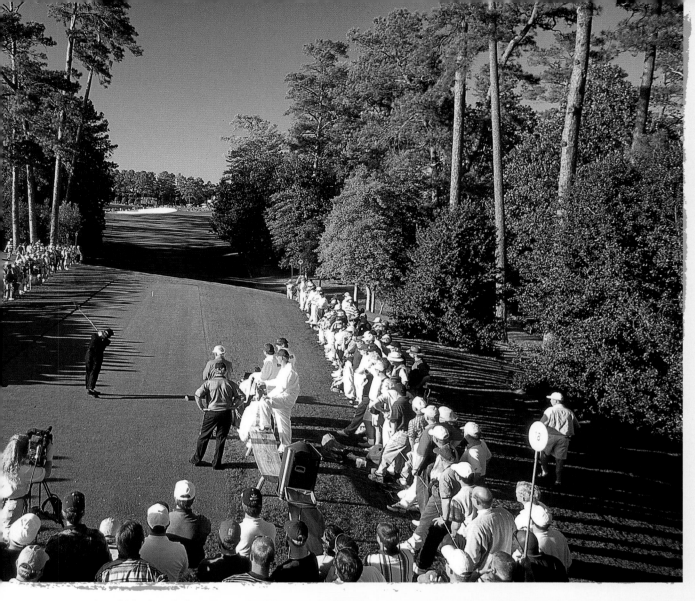

LEFT
Gary Player in action
on the 18th tee at the
2000 US Masters.

FAR LEFT
Gary Player kisses the
Open trophy on his
third win in 1974.

crowd could be heard cheering. At the first play-off hole both men were faced with tricky putts for par and, this time, some of Jacklin's fans disturbed Player just as he was about to strike his crucial putt. The South African may have been seething but he composed himself and waited for the crowd to settle down before holing out and piling the pressure on his opponent. Jacklin duly missed his short putt and the match was over.

As this episode highlights, Gary Player was undoubtedly one of the toughest competitors the game has ever seen. Dressed in black, he appeared utterly single-minded in his determination to win. By paying close attention to his diet and taking regular, strenuous exercise Player was also able to compete at the highest level well into his 40s. In fact, his last major triumph

came at the Masters in 1978 when he was 42. Heading into the final round Player was seven shots adrift of the leader Hubert Green with other big names such as Nicklaus, Ballesteros, Watson and Trevino also in the hunt. But despite the pedigree of his younger opponents it was Player who accelerated to the top of the leaderboard shooting a remarkable 30 for the last nine holes to complete a sparkling round of 64.

Gary Player's risky decision to leave a comfortable life in South Africa and follow in the footsteps of Bobby Locke paid off because he would never accept failure. His positive mental outlook was perhaps his greatest asset, enabling him to compete consistently in four separate decades and become one of the few to capture golf's four greatest prizes.

NICK**PRICE**

Born: Durban, South Africa January 28, 1957
Turned professional: 1977
Open: Winner in 1994, 2nd in 1988, tied 2nd in 1982
USPGA: Winner in 1992, 1994

When he was at the peak of his playing powers, Nick Price could beat anyone, and he often did. Indeed, the quality of his short game was such that many observers believe he could, on his day, have beaten any of the greats in golf's history. There was an all-too-brief period, between 1992 and 1994, when the Zimbabwean mowed down just about everyone in his path. Of the 54 tournaments he played, Price walked away with the winner's cheque for 16 – almost a one-in-three strike rate. And that purple patch included the three major championships he claimed during his career as well as the Players Championship in 1993.

But that incredible run had been a long time coming: Price had joined the professional game way back in 1977, and had won his first European Tour event in 1982. And after 1994, the victories started to dry up, before vanishing completely after 2002.

It's doubtful that we've seen the last of Nick Price; it just would have been nice to have seen more of him at his very best. His trophy tally could almost certainly have been more than the three majors, 18 PGA Tour tournaments, six European Tour events and sundry other titles he can currently boast.

Price was born in South Africa to English parents but later became a citizen of Zimbabwe. And it was in Zimbabwe, around the age of eight, that he discovered his natural aptitude for hitting golf balls into little cups. He soon outgrew the competition in his native land, and found wider acclaim at the age of 17 when he won the Junior World Championship in San Diego, California in 1974.

Young Price turned professional in 1977, when he was 20, spent some time on the European Tour and won his first tournament, the Swiss Open, in 1980. Next it was off to the PGA Tour, where he made an immediate impact by winning the 1983 World Series of Golf. There then followed, however, a long period when little was heard or seen of him, apart from a near miss at the 1988 Open.

Price had worked hard at his swing, and had taken advice from the likes of golf guru David Leadbetter. When he re-emerged from his eight-year barren spell by winning the 1991 Byron Nelson Classic, the world found a new star.

The following year Price, by now aged 35, found himself at Bellerive Country Club, St Louis, Missouri, chasing down the flagging Gene Sauers in the final round of the PGA Championship. It was a late, late run for the finishing line – Price took the lead for the first time at the 222-yard 16th, when he lined up a birdie by hitting a 2-iron to within 25 feet – but it counted. Pars on the final two holes meant he had won his first major by three strokes. And the wins started to flow.

A highly successful year in 1993, when he won four times in America, led the PGA money list and won the Vardon Trophy, was really only an appetiser for what was to follow in 1994.

In the Open Championship of that year, played at Turnberry, a crowd of players were jostling for top spot as the final day dawned. Price was among them, tied for third place with Jesper Parnevik, Ronan Rafferty and

Tom Watson. One by one the challengers fell away, and it was left to Price and Parnevik to battle it out over the back nine. It was nip and tuck all the way, but Parnevik had good reason to believe the Open was his when he stood two strokes in front after the 17th. Behind him, however, Price was working miracles.

Not content with a birdie at the 16th, he miraculously holed a 50-footer for an eagle at the 17th, leaving Parnevik needing to par the final hole to win or tie. Unfortunately for the Swede, he thought he needed a birdie and attacked the hole rather too aggressively, taking a bogey five. Now Price could win by finishing with a par four, and he calmly did so.

Weeks later, Price had his sights set on a second PGA Championship win at Southern Hills in Oklahoma, and he accomplished it in brilliant style. After dominating a staggeringly strong field from the first day, he scored a fantastic final-round 67, setting a new 72-hole record of 271 for a US major championship. He had become the first player to win majors back to back since Tom Watson in 1982.

Sad to say, it was a feat Nick Price never looked like repeating. That PGA was his last major championship, and in fact he did not win another PGA tournament until three years had elapsed. As with so many other golfers, fans were left wondering what might have been.

Legends of **GOLF**

GENE**SARAZEN**

Born: New York, USA February 27, 1902

Died: May 13, 1999

Turned professional: 1920

Masters: Winner in 1935

US Open: Winner in 1922, 1932

Open: Winner in 1932

USPGA: Winner in 1922, 1923, 1933

Ryder Cup record: Member of 6 US teams (1927, 1929, 1931, 1933, 1935, 1937). Played 12, Won 7, Lost 2, Halved 3

When Gene Sarazen won the Masters in 1935 he became the first golfer to complete the Grand Slam. At just 5ft 3ins tall Sarazen was a diminutive figure with an intense determination that drove his career for over half a century. His list of triumphs dates back to the US Open of 1922, and he remained competitive into his 70s. Sarazen's story is one that reveals hard graft and skill in equal measures.

Sarazen's willingness to make the most of his natural talent as a golfer can be traced back to his early years, growing up in Harrison, New York. Born Eugeni Sarazani in 1902, he was the son of Italian immigrants and his upbringing was far from privileged. By the age of eight, he was caddying at a local country club to supplement the family income. He left school at 15 and moved with his family to Connecticut where he worked as an apprentice in a factory. Labouring in difficult conditions Sarazen contracted pleurisy and his doctor recommended that he should work outside to accelerate his recuperation. He soon found a job at Brooklawn Country Club where his duties included making clubs and generally helping the resident professional.

By 17 he had changed his name to the more American sounding "Gene" and was earning his wage as an assistant professional. When he arrived at the Skokie Country Club, Illinois, to compete in the 1922 US Open he was an unknown 20-year-old but despite his tender years and relative inexperience, Sarazen became the first player to break 70 in the final round to win. His sparkling 68 included a birdie

on the final hole after hitting his second shot approach to the par-5 with a driver. The exciting and fearless fashion of his first major victory propelled Sarazen into the limelight and later that year he won the USPGA to kick-start his career at the top level with an incredible bang.

In 1923 Sarazen won the USPGA for the second time, but this would be his last major triumph until the Open of 1932. This hiatus divides his record into two distinct phases and can be blamed on two factors – the emergence of Bobby Jones and a growing concern over his technique. Sarazen was a small man with a compact swing that lacked the rhythmic beauty of his great contemporary. He employed an interlocking hold and his left thumb had a tendency to fly away from the grip during the swing. Despite some respectable results during a period in which he worked hard to rectify the

GENE**SARAZEN**

faults, Sarazen lacked the self-confidence to succeed under intense pressure.

He finally returned to the winner's circle in 1932 with victory at the Open by an emphatic five shots over fellow American Macdonald Smith. His four round total of 283 was a record that remained unbeaten until Bobby Locke scored 279 at Troon in 1950. Sarazen then crossed the Atlantic to claim the US Open crown at Fresh Meadow in New York. In keeping with the style of his victory 10 years earlier he shot 66 on the final day to win by three, playing the final 28 holes in a staggering 100 shots.

Sarazen's seventh and final major title came in 1935 at the US Masters, where his influence over the back

18
393 YDS
BOGEY 5

nine helped create its modern day reputation for being the most dangerous stretch in the game. Standing on the par-5 15th tee of his final round, Sarazen was three shots behind an imperious Craig Wood. He followed a long, straight drive with a 4-wood approach that found the bottom of the cup. This incredible albatross enabled Sarazen to force a play-off that he eventually won by five strokes.

The Masters of 1935 was Sarazen's last great triumph although he remained a serious competitor for another four decades. During the Open of 1973 at Troon (50 years after his debut in the event) he scored a hole-in-one at the 8th on his way to shooting an impressive round of 79.

Like many of his contemporaries, Sarazen's achievements stretched beyond competition, and he is credited with the design of the modern sand wedge after he realised that by building up the sole, the clubhead would maintain its momentum as it bounced through sand. This discovery suddenly made bunker shots an easier proposition as players could hit aggressively behind the ball and still expect to see it emerge onto the green. He also presented the popular television show, "Shell's Wonderful World of Golf" that brought many of the game's great players together in head-to-head battles. By the time of his death in 1999 at the age of 97, Gene Sarazen had left an indelible mark on the game he cherished.

VIJAY SINGH

Born: Lautoke, Fiji February 22, 1963
Turned professional: 1982
Masters: Winner in 2000
US Open: Tied 3rd in 1999
Open: Tied 2nd in 2003
USPGA: Winner in 1998, 2004

On September 6th, 2004, 41-year-old Vijay Singh won the Deutsche Bank Championship in Boston and ended Tiger Woods' 264-week reign as the best golfer in the world. He remains the only player to have consistently challenged Woods, never doubting his ability to beat his great opponent when it really mattered. His achievements, including three major championships, have been founded on a combination of natural talent and old-fashioned hard graft. And it is this work ethic that enabled Singh to leave his native Fiji with a game good enough to compete against high calibre fields all around the world.

When Vijay Singh turned professional in 1982 he knew that success on the Asian Tour would have to come thick and, more importantly, fast to make it as a player. Growing up in Nadi, Fiji, Singh did not have the sort of structured golfing education afforded to players in the American university system. Instead, his father, an airplane technician and part-time golf instructor, was responsible for Singh's development as a player and encouraged his son to pursue his early infatuation with the game. So at the age of 19 Singh set about travelling through Asia scraping a living on Tour. His breakthrough victory came two years later at the Malaysian PGA. This win confirmed the Fijian's talent and finally vindicated his brave decision to play competitively for a living.

Despite the consistent success that followed, Singh's ascent to the major Tours proved to be a difficult journey. At the 1985 Indonesian Open he was accused of altering the score on his card and despite professing his innocence was suspended from the Asian Tour for two years. For a player beginning to make his mark this was a bitter blow as he was forced to retire to Borneo to become a club professional. But the financial security of a steady job enabled Singh to save enough money to resurrect his career and he did not have to wait long for success. On his return he won the 1988 Nigerian Open and soon qualified to compete on the European Tour.

Over the next four years Singh was a regular winner in Europe and in 1993 he graduated to the US Tour. Having captured the Buick Classic, defeating Mark Wiebe in a play-off, Singh was named PGA Tour Rookie of the Year. Back and neck injuries may have hampered his progress the following season but facing fierce competition week after week was making the Fijian a resolute competitor.

BELOW
Singh at the US Masters 2006.

VIJAY**SINGH**

In 1998, aged 35, Vijay Singh became a major winner. The venue for the USPGA Championship was the 6,906-yard, par 70 layout at Sahalee in Seattle. Throughout the week Singh's game was a model of consistency and he added scores of 66, 67 and 68 to his opening round of 70 to take the title by two shots from American Steve Stricker. Two years later he picked up the Green Jacket, defeating Ernie Els by three shots after a spectacular final round 69.

Moving towards his 40s Vijay Singh could have been forgiven for relaxing the intensive practice regime that had become his trademark, but he continued to work just as hard as ever to close the gap between himself and Tiger Woods. His devotion paid off spectacularly in 2003 when he recorded a staggering 18 top 10 finishes,

LEFT
Singh tees off from the prestigious mega-project 'The World' in Dubai.

FAR LEFT
Vijay Singh wins the Masters in 2000.

including four tournament victories. This amazing run coincided with a dip in form from Woods and the Fijian ended the season on top of the moneylist, having won almost $1 million more than his great rival.

But the glory of 2003 was just a teaser for what was about to unfold. He won nine times in 2004, including his second USPGA Championship in a play-off against Chris DiMarco and Justin Leonard at Whistling Straits. The 42-year-old amassed over $10 million in prize money and, crucially, took Tiger's world number one crown. For the first time in seven years there was a new name at the top of the golfing world.

But through this period of domination controversy was never far away and Singh was heavily criticised in all areas of the media. In 2003, Annika Sorenstam accepted

an invitation to play on the PGA Tour, much to Singh's frustration. He felt that she was taking the place of a journeyman player trying to make a living and his rash comments were construed by many as sexist.

Then there is the prickly relationship between himself and Woods which was sparked at the President's Cup of 2000 when Singh's caddie wore a baseball cap that read, "Tiger who?" Woods felt this to be disrespectful and as the Fijian passed the American in the world rankings their encounters remained hostile.

And yet despite these controversies, Singh commands respect for making the most of his God-given talent and emerging from the pack to become the only successful challenger to the great Tiger Woods.

Legends of **GOLF**

SAM**SNEAD**

Born: Hot Springs, Virginia, USA May 27, 1912
Died: May 23, 2002
Turned professional: 1934
Masters: Winner in 1949, 1952, 1954
US Open: 2nd in 1932, 1947, 1953
Open: Winner in 1946
USPGA: Winner in 1942, 1949, 1951
Ryder Cup record: Member of 7 US teams (1937, 1947, 1949, 1951, 1953, 1955, 1959). Played 13, Won 10, Lost 2, Halved 1. Captain in 1951, 1959, 1969

The age-old golfing proverb 'it's not how but how many', which places low scores above perfect methods, is sound advice. However, given the choice any golfer would love to swing with the same brand of power and elegance that became the signature of **Samuel Jackson Snead. His instinctively smooth style has led many to believe that the man from Virginia was, in fact, the most talented the sport has ever seen. But whilst his record of seven major championships remains a glorious testament to his great ability, it falls some way short of the achievements of Nicklaus, Palmer, Hogan and Woods. Despite his immense talent (he was the first player to shoot 59 in competition) "Slamming Sam's" Achilles heel was his mental application.**

Sam Snead was born in May 1912 near the town of Hot Springs in the backwaters of Virginia. His family owned a small plot of land and Snead, along with his five brothers, would lend his hand to various odd jobs including milling and chicken tending. At school he had a reputation as a talented sportsman, playing baseball, basketball and football to a decent standard. But it was only when he left full-time education and secured a job working at his local course that he started playing golf regularly. Through these early years Snead developed his own unique style and quickly emerged as a player of serious note. In fact, the strength of his performances led to a move to the wealthier Greenbrier Club at White Sulphur Springs. Here his education as a player continued as he caddied for,

and then taught, the club's members. Snead clearly made a serious impact on the Greenbrier regulars as in 1936 they clubbed together to finance his attempts to make it on Tour.

With just $300 to his name he knew that to continue competing he would have to record some top finishes, and fast. He duly won the Oakland Open on his third start, pocketing a cheque for $1,200 in the process.

This kick-started a professional career that spanned an incredible six decades, during which time Snead was a regular winner. He claimed his first major title in 1942 at the USPGA, which at the time was a matchplay championship, defeating Jim Turnesa in the final by 2&1.

His next Major victory came at St. Andrews in the Open of 1946. Throughout his career Snead competed very few times outside America and only travelled to

BELOW
Honorary starter Sam Snead at the 2002 Masters.

play in the Open on three occasions. In 1937 he finished tied 11th at Carnoustie and when he returned to the Fife coast nine years later was relatively green in the intricacies of Scottish seaside golf. And yet despite this inexperience, and a burning dislike for the course, he prevailed by four strokes in typically strong winds, proving his natural class. But sadly for the British public he only made one more appearance in the Open, an unremarkable sixth-placed finish at Troon in 1962.

In America, however, Snead was a consistent challenger when the major prizes were handed out. His third and final Masters title in 1954 pitted him against one of his greatest adversaries, Ben Hogan, in an 18-hole play-off. With a deft touch on the greens to compliment his high quality ball striking Snead defeated his

illustrious opponent by one stroke. His three wins in the
USPGA further underline just how adept he was in
head-to-head confrontations.

And yet for a player of such outstanding talent there
remains a large gap in his impressive CV. Snead threw
everything he had at the US Open but despite finishing
in the top 10 on ten occasions (including four times as
runner-up) he never won and the tournament became
an albatross around his neck. The tone was set in 1937
when he made his US Open debut, finishing two shots
behind Ralph Guldahl at Oakland Hills. Unfortunately
for Snead, he would come even closer without winning
in 1939. Needing a par-5 on the final hole at Spring Hill
in Philadelphia to win he was caught in a greenside
bunker before three putting and registering a triple

bogey eight. Then, eight years later, he missed a putt of
around 4ft to continue his play-off with Lew Worsham.

For all his natural ability, Snead was a
temperamental player and many felt that in certain
circumstances he lacked important tactical awareness.
But the fact that he was an open character with
tangible flaws doubtless contributed to his popularity.
Snead was a rural boy, a hillbilly at heart, with such an
attractive style that he inevitably drew comparisons with
Bobby Jones.

Sam Snead died in 2002 as the most prolific winner
the US Tour had ever seen. Dubbed, 'Slammin Sam' for
his dynamic and powerful swing, he, above any other
on this list, was perhaps blessed with the greatest God-
given talent.

ANNIKA**SORENSTAM**

Annika Sorenstam is without question the greatest female golfer of the modern era. Just as Tiger Woods has dominated the men's game, Sorenstam has left a glorious legacy, a crucial chapter in the history of the women's game. Ally to her deadly accurate ball striking she has the sort of mental strength that drives her game when under pressure and breathes fear into the hearts of those around her on the leaderboard. Her current tally of nine major championships, that includes victories in each of the big four, is an achievement that no other player in the modern era has come close to matching.

Annika Sorenstam was born into a sports-mad family in Stockholm in October 1970 but it was tennis, not golf, which received the lion's share of her attention growing up. Both Annika and her sister Charlotte reached a high standard within the junior ranks in Sweden but a weak backhand became a frustrating hurdle that Annika was unable to overcome and so she slowly began to devote more of her attention to golf. Under the guidance of Swedish coach Henri Reiss she developed the key fundamentals for a solid long game and, aged 19, travelled to America to enroll at the University of Arizona where she soon made her mark on the amateur game. In 1992 she played in the winning World Amateur Team Championships and realised a dream by qualifying for the US Open at Oakmont. It was the crowning moment in a glorious amateur career that inspired her to turn pro.

Annika Sorenstam took to life on Tour with ease and finished her rookie season in third place on the European Tour's Order of Merit. This initial success paved the way for her to take up membership of the USLPGA Tour in 1994 and a steady season was rewarded with a place on the European Solheim Cup team for the clash at The Greenbrier Golf Club in West Virginia. Sorenstam performed solidly in a losing team and announced herself on the international stage.

But her major breakthrough came in 1995. At the start of the US Tour season she was a regular top 10 finisher and in June she travelled to Europe where she proceeded to win twice. Heading into the US Open at Broadmoor Golf Club in Colorado she was at the top of her game. A sparkling opening round 67 was followed by two scores in the 70s and Sorenstam found herself trailing Meg Mallon by five strokes going into the final day. But the 24-year-old shot a closing round of 68 to pile the pressure on her more experienced opponent. Mallon's game then crumbled under the heat, leaving her Swedish challenger one shot clear at the top of the leaderboard.

Born: Stockholm, Sweden October 9, 1970

Turned professional: 1992

Kraft Nabisco Championship: Winner in 2001, 2002, 2005

LPGA Championship: Winner in 2003, 2004, 2005

US Women's Open: Winner in 1995, 1996

Du Maurier Classic/Women's British Open: Winner in 2003

Solheim cup record: Member of 7 European teams (1994, 1996, 1998, 2000, 2002, 2003, 2005). Played 27, Won 16, Lost 8, Halved 3

ANNIKA**SORENSTAM**

new challenge in 2003 and by entering The Colonial tournament at Fort Worth became the first female to compete on the premier men's Tour since Babe Zaharias in 1945. Under intense media scrutiny she finished five over par and missed the cut but, despite failing to make the weekend, proved that her game was strong enough to take on the men.

Annika Sorenstam's record of nine major victories is the single most outstanding achievement in the women's game. Thirteen years after making her debut as a touring professional she still has an unwavering determination to add to her list of achievements. By the end of her career there will be a new benchmark against which all future superstars will be judged.

Sorenstam successfully defended her US Open crown in 1996 by a staggering eight shot margin, cementing her status as the dominant force within the women's game. But then, just as the Swede appeared to be in a class of her own, the major victories suddenly dried up. For five years she competed successfully on Tour without clinching any of the big four and Australian Karrie Webb emerged to take her crown as the number one golfer in the world.

In 2001 Annika Sorenstam realised that to fulfil her considerable potential she needed to dedicate herself to the game like she had done at the start of her career. A strict physical training regime was complemented by sheer hard work on the range and her results immediately picked up. On her way to victory at the Standard Register PING tournament she became the first female professional to break 60 in competition and then returned to the major winner's circle with victory at the LPGA Nabisco Championship. She finished the 2001 season with eight victories and over two million dollars to her name.

Since then Sorenstam has won countless Tour titles and at least one major every year. Then, having scaled the heights of the women's game, she sought a brand

PAYNE
STEWART

Born: Springfield, Massachusetts, USA January 30, 1957

Died: October 25, 1999

Turned professional: 1979

Masters: Tied 8th in 1986

US Open: Winner in 1991, 1999

Open: Second in 1985

USPGA: Winner in 1989

Ryder Cup record: Member of 5 US teams (1987, 1989, 1991, 1993, 1999) Played 19, Won 7, Lost 10, Halved 2

Dressed in plus fours, tam-o-shanter hat and psychedelic socks, Payne Stewart always cut the most recognisable figure on the golf course. His was a dashing game built on an elegance and style that justified his eye-catching outfits and endeared him to galleries around the world. His three major victories succeeded countless near misses as he learnt the art of winning through the pain of defeat. But Stewart never bemoaned bad luck and his genuine sportsmanship made him popular among his fellow professionals. When he died tragically in 1999, at the age of 42, the golfing world mourned the loss of one of its dearest sons.

Payne Stewart was introduced to the game at the age of four by his father Bill Stewart, an accomplished player in his own right who had won the Missouri State Amateur Championship and qualified to play in the 1955 US Open. Under Bill's guidance Payne developed as a serious player, earning a place on the South Methodist University golf team. But when he turned professional in 1979 he was far from being the polished international performer that he later became. He chose to ply his trade on the Asian Tour where he learnt the art of building a score under pressure, and victories in India and Indonesia were crucial to financing his travels as well as his development as a golfer.

But after finally earning his playing privileges for the US Tour in 1982 Stewart developed an unwanted reputation as a choker. After narrow misses in the 1985 Opens of America and Britain he led with six holes to play at the 1986 Shinnecock Hills US Open but was outmuscled by the more experienced Ray

Floyd. By this time his reputation as 'the best player never to have won a major preceded him. But he remained adamant that he had the mental strength to become a major winner and in 1989 captured the USPGA Championship at Kemper Lakes. The manner of this victory proved beyond doubt that he was a gritty fighter capable of producing his best golf just when he needed it the most. With nine holes left to play Stewart sat five shots behind the leader, Mike Reid, but applied the pressure by making five birdies over the final seven holes for a spectacular back nine score of 31. Reid faltered during the closing stretch and Stewart became a major winner, aged 32.

Two years later at Hazeltine, Minnesota, he again made crucial birdies at the death to force a play-off with Scott Simpson for the US Open. The extra-time head-to-head was memorable as an exhibition of bitter determination by Stewart. His game had fragmented overnight and he was forced to rely on a deft touch around the greens, scraping together a score of 75 to beat Simpson by two.

BELOW
Stewart in Ryder Cup action, 1987.

Payne Stewart made five Ryder Cup appearances in total, winning seven matches and losing 10. After taking points in each of his five matches on debut in 1987 Stewart remained an ever present in the US team until 1993. But after the American team tasted victory at the Belfry Stewart's form dipped and he was forced to sit out the next two encounters. In 1999, after a spiritual awakening had encouraged him to re-dedicate himself to his family and his career, Stewart returned to form with a victory at the start of the season at Pebble Beach.

That year the US Open was held at Pinehurst, a narrow tree-lined course that places a premium on accurate ball striking and a patient gameplan. Over the last nine holes an exciting duel between Stewart and Phil of sportsmanship. When it became clear that the US had won the cup Stewart conceded his match to the Scot who had faced a tirade of abuse from the crowd throughout the afternoon. On a day when many American players damaged their reputations, Stewart showed a selfless disregard for his own record and had the integrity to put his own ambitions to one side.

Just one month after the clash at Brookline the golfing world was rocked as Stewart tragically died on board a Learjet flying between Orlando and Texas. A gradual loss of cabin pressure was to blame for the hypoxia that killed everyone on board. After cruising on autopilot the plane finally ran out of fuel and crashed into a field in Aberdeen, South Dakota.

Payne Stewart's infectious character and striking wardrobe were responsible for injecting colour and sportsmanship into golf. His sudden death was a devastating blow that came at the end of a sparkling renaissance season in which he returned to the major winner's circle after an eight year hiatus.

LEFT
Stewart displays his plus-fours in the 1990 Open at St. Andrews.

FAR LEFT
Stewart played in the 1999 Ryder Cup, it was to be his last.

BELOW
Payne Stewart, 1999 US Open Champion.

Mickelson emerged. The damp and dingy conditions had made scoring tough and by keeping their scores intact Mickelson and Stewart had detached from the field. On the 17th tee there was nothing between them, although a precise 6-iron approach allowed Stewart to make a birdie and take a one shot lead. But a wayward drive on the par-4 18th forced him to lay up short of the green and a play-off seemed inevitable when his pitch finished 15ft from the pin. Payne Stewart proceeded to hole the longest ever putt to win the US Open.

This spectacular victory earned him a place on Ben Crenshaw's infamous 1999 Ryder Cup side at Brookline. Playing at the end of the singles field against Colin Montgomerie, Stewart performed an unprecedented act

CURTIS**STRANGE**

It's odd, isn't it, how golfers, having reached for the stars and found them within their reach, suddenly stop winning. It's happened to more than one legend of golf featured within these pages, and you couldn't find a better example of the phenomenon than Curtis Strange.

Strange won 17 times on the PGA Tour, with the first victory coming in 1979 and the last in 1989. And guess what tournament that final win came in. It was the US Open Championship. Talk about going out on a high.

The Virginian had blazed a trail like a comet across the Tour for 10 years, and his haul of four trophies in 1988 included his first US Open. But after 1989, nothing except the occasional non-Tour title came his way, and Strange finally left pro golf to concentrate on a broadcasting career.

Now he's back, competing on the Champions Tour, but his 2006 season saw him reaching no higher than 52nd on the money list, and memories of him in those halcyon days will remain just that: memories.

Strange was at an advantage in his childhood in that his father owned White Sands Country Club in Virginia Beach, Virginia, and it was natural for the boy to pick up golf clubs and start swinging. The early start began to pay off when he won the Virginia Junior Championship at the age of 15.

Later, at Wake Forest University, he had the good fortune to play in the same collegiate team as future PGA Tour professionals Jay Haas and Bob Byman, and what a team that must have been. Indeed, Golf World called the Wake Forest players of 1974 and 1975 "the greatest college team of all time". And it was in 1974 that Strange collected the World Amateur Cup.

It was a logical move when he turned professional in 1976, and Strange's first win on the PGA Tour came along in 1979, when he triumphed at the Pensacola Open. The stream of victories in the following years was steady rather than spectacular, but he seemed to be preparing for great things when he won three Tour events in 1987, having already topped the money list in 1985.

So it proved. Strange was at the top of the money list again in 1988, and he became the first golfer to bank cheques worth more than $1 million from the Tour in a single season. He picked up four pieces of silverware that year, and among them was the venerated US Open Championship trophy.

It was no stroll in the park for Strange, nor was it for Nick Faldo, his opponent in the 18-hole play-off that

Born: Norfolk, Virginia, USA January 30, 1955
Turned professional: 1976
Masters: Tied 2nd in 1985
US Open: Winner in 1988, 1989, 3rd in 1984
Ryder Cup record: Member of 5 US teams (1983, 1985, 1987, 1989, 1995). Played 20, Won 6, Lost 12, Halved 2. Captain in 2002

There were no such problems for Strange, who parred the first 15 holes and had opened up a two-stroke lead over Mark McCumber, Chip Beck and Ian Woosnam by the time he got to the 17th tee. He could afford himself the luxury of a bogey at the 18th and still win by a stroke.

And there, at the Oak Hill Country Club in Rochester, New York, Curtis Strange's winning run on the PGA Tour ended: strange but true. Let us not forget, he was a determined competitor and a truly talented golfer, as those who saw his course record 62 at St. Andrews in the 1987 Dunhill Cup will testify. It's just odd that it all fell away so dramatically.

decided the title. Nevertheless, Strange came out on top by the impressive margin of four strokes. It had been a two-man battle from the fourth round, with the lead changing hands several times, and it was no great surprise when the two golfers were level after 72 holes.

By halfway in the play-off, Strange had pulled into a one-stroke advantage. The lead kept growing, Faldo did not help his cause when he bogeyed three of the final four holes, and Strange was left clutching the trophy.

Few people have won back-to-back major tournaments, but our man can claim that distinction. A year after dismissing Faldo's challenge, he was back on the winner's podium at the US Open, the first man to win consecutive Opens for 38 years.

Shooting 71 in the first round, on a day when 21 men broke par 70, Strange stood five strokes behind the leaders. Day two was distinguished by no fewer than four players scoring holes in one within 90 minutes of each other, and it also saw Strange shoot a marvellous 64 and take first place on the leaderboard, one stroke ahead of Tom Kite.

Heavy rain affected the third day's play, and it also disturbed Strange, who ended with a 73 and fell to third place, three strokes behind Kite. However, the final round was not to be Kite's day and he struck a problem-filled 78, dropping to ninth place.

JH**TAYLOR**

Born: Devon, England March 19, 1871
Died: February 10, 1963
Turned professional: 1890
US Open: 2nd in 1900
Open: Winner in 1894, 1895, 1900, 1909, 1913
Ryder Cup record: Captain in 1933

The youngest member of the "Great Triumvirate", John Henry Taylor was the first to make a serious breakthrough in the sport. His victory in the 1894 Open Championship at St. George's was the first by a player from outside Scotland. Building on this initial success he won the event on four more occasions and finished second a staggering five times. By his death in 1963 he had been a leading figure in the game, both on and off the course for almost a century.

JH Taylor was born and bred in the South West and by the age of 11 had started his golfing education by caddying for members at his local course in North Devon. As he watched accomplished golfers wrestling with this rugged links he learned that to build a decent score, especially in the wind, precise ball control was critical. As he began playing himself he developed a compact swing that squared the clubface regularly through impact. A solid technique led to some impressive performances and his reputation as a talented teenager grew quickly as he competed regularly for the Northam men's working club. At the age of 21 he secured a job as the first professional at Burnham and Berrow Golf Club in Somerset where he also fulfilled the role as greenkeeper.

The following year, Taylor showed his class by beating the respected St. Andrews professional Andrew Kirkaldy. As the Open at Prestwick loomed, JH Taylor was regarded as one of the field's most dangerous competitors despite never having experienced the unique pressure of the event. He duly

confirmed his pre-tournament billing by shooting a record low 75 in the opening round but this was followed by a disappointing 89 in poor weather and Taylor's chances had all but gone. He eventually finished in a respectable, yet disappointing 10th place.

But Taylor would not have to wait long for the breakthrough he craved and in 1894 the Championship travelled south of the border for the first time to Sandwich in Kent. Taylor's shotmaking was too much for the rest of the field (he was the first player to use lofted irons, like wedges, to attack greens) and his winning score of 326 was five shots better than Douglas Rolland in second. The first English venue provided the first English winner and JH Taylor had joined an elite group of players at golf's top table.

The following year Taylor showed his tenacity by recovering from an opening round 86 to remain in the hunt for the title. As the weather deteriorated through

BELOW
Taylor pictured in 1945.

the final day the leader, Sandy Herd, faced St. Andrews at its meanest and Taylor emerged victorious by four strokes.

His second consecutive victory confirmed Taylor as the leading player of the time, but the emergence of Harry Vardon meant that he would have to wait five years before capturing his third Open crown.

In 1899 JH Taylor left his post at Burnham to take on the professional's job at Royal Mid Surrey, a course that was constructed under his guidance. Despite being an inland venue – close to London – Taylor was able to construct a course that reflected many of the traits that define and defend the challenge at Royal North Devon. Not a long course, Royal Mid Surrey still favours imaginative shotmakers able to negotiate a safe passage

LEFT
Taylor on the putting green, 1908.

FAR LEFT
John Henry Taylor poses before a game, 1908.

through the fierce rough and trees that line the fairways. Taylor remained the professional there until his retirement in 1946.

In the same year that Taylor joined Royal Mid Surrey he also crossed the Atlantic to play in the US Open. Not for the first time, he finished second to Harry Vardon – the two taking their rivalry to an appreciative American crowd. The battle between them re-commenced later that year at St. Andrews and this time it was Taylor's turn to take the prize as he won his third Open title, beating Vardon by eight shots and James Braid by 13.

Between Taylor's first major triumph in 1894 and the start of World War I the "Great Triumvirate" dominated golf, providing the public with a fierce rivalry that served to raise the profile of the sport. Taylor prevailed in the

Open on two more occasions in 1909 and 1913 and his other major achievements included winning the Matchplay Championship in 1908 and captaining the winning Great Britain and Ireland side in the 1933 Ryder Cup.

Like many of the great players featured in this book Taylor's impact stretched further than his achievements as a player. He became an accomplished course architect, lending his experienced eye to notable layouts such as Royal Birkdale and Machrihanish. He was also a major influence in the foundation of the Professional Golfers Association, an organisation that still works to uphold the interests of professional golfers. By the time he died at the age of 91, he had given back to the game just as much as he had taken.

Legends of **GOLF**

PETER**THOMSON**

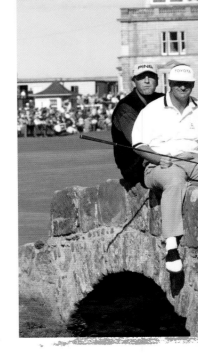

In 1954, Peter Thomson became the first Australian to win a major. He was an intelligent golfer with an acute strategic sense and a solid all-round game. In the heat of the battle Thomson would remain unfazed, focused on delivering the perfect shot at exactly the right moment. And it was this unique trait that marked him out as a player of supreme talent. Between 1952 and 1958 no British golfer finished above him in the Open and he won the Championship four times. When he added a fifth title in 1965, he confirmed his status as a true master of the links.

The details of Peter Thomson's early career are somewhat sketchy but it is widely accepted that his initial intention was to become a chemist. When he finished as the top amateur in the Australian Open of 1948, however, it was clear that his future lay within golf. He turned pro in 1949 and, just like Bobby Locke 11 years before, Thomson made an immediate impact as a full-time player. He won the 1950 New Zealand Open and finished second in the Australian Open later that year. At this time a victory in Australasia would be worth far less than triumph in America but Thomson realised the need to prove himself at home – something he did in 1951 when he claimed the first of his three Australian Open titles.

It was not until 1953 that Thomson broadened his horizons and took to the States. He started a regular routine that would see him play in America during the early part of the season before returning to his homeland every July. Between 1953 and 1959, he had 42 top 10 finishes in America, including victory in the Texas Open and a fourth place finish in the US Open in 1956. The following year he finished fourth in the Masters but as Thomson reached his 30s, his trips to the States became more sporadic. For such a talented player, his limited success in America can be credited to the target golf style courses that place a premium on power off the tee and aggressive tactics. This was never the Australian's style and he found himself more at home on the naturally crafted courses of the European Tour.

Peter Thomson and Bobby Locke may have been born on separate continents, 12 years apart, but their careers collided during a sparkling decade from 1949 in which they finished first or second in the Open twelve times. At the start of this period of dual dominance there was no doubt who was the more established player. Locke was a prolific winner on the US Tour and had also made his name in Europe. But Thomson's

Born: Melbourne, Australia August 23, 1929
Turned professional: 1949
Masters: 5th in 1957
US Open: 4th 1956
Open: Winner in 1954, 1955, 1956, 1958, 1965

could be so prolific in Britain yet fail to make such an emphatic impact in the US. He again crushed any lingering American murmurs at the age of 55 when he won 10 times in one season on the US Seniors Tour.

Peter Thomson became the first Australian to reach the pinnacle of his profession. Dressed conservatively in dark clothes and white shoes he was a calm competitor who moved serenely around the course, unaffected by the pressure of crucial situations. His influence was to prove that Australian players had the ability to win at the highest level and the likes of Greg Norman, David Graham and Adam Scott have since continued this legacy.

LEFT
Peter Thomson along with Mark Calcavecchia, Sandy Lyle and Mark O'Meara in the Champions Challenge at St. Andrews in 2000.

BELOW
Thomson on the practice ground at the Open, Royal Birkdale 1965.

game was better suited to the unique challenge of the Open and he went one better than his South African counterpart by winning the Championship five times.

When the 1954 Open travelled to Royal Birkdale, Bobby Locke was bidding for his third title. Thomson was yet to make his mark but captured the Claret Jug by finishing one stroke ahead of the South African. Winning the Open and beating Locke in a tight head-to-head battle instilled the confidence in Thomson that kick-started his domination of the event. His victories in the next two championships making him the first player to complete three consecutive wins since Bob Ferguson 74 years earlier.

Perhaps Thomson's greatest achievement, however, was his last Open triumph in 1965. Seven years after winning his fourth at St. Andrews, the 35-year-old was competing in a high quality field that included Arnold Palmer, Tony Lima and Jack Nicklaus. The Australian hung on to a slender two shot lead over Christie O'Connor with nerveless long iron approach shots to the final two greens. Throughout his Open career pressure seemed to draw the best from Thomson and this was no more apparent than at the death of the 1965 tournament.

His last major victory also served to silence critics in America who had questioned the calibre of the Open fields, struggling to understand how Thomson

LEE**TREVINO**

Born: Dallas, Texas, USA December 1, 1939

Turned professional: 1960

Masters: 10th in 1975

US Open: Winner in 1968, 1971

Open: Winner in 1971, 1972

USPGA: Winner in 1974, 1984

Ryder Cup record: Member of 6 US teams (1969, 1971, 1973, 1975, 1979, 1981). Played 30, Won 17, Lost 7, Halved 6. Captain in 1985

It is impossible to talk about Lee Trevino without emphasising the financial difficulties that punctuated his formative years. Many of the players featured in this book, such as Ben Hogan, Sam Snead and Gene Sarazen, rose to prominence from underprivileged beginnings but for Trevino golf was a means to scrape a few essential dollars to survive. As a hustler he developed a confident, talkative style that remained part of his infectious character throughout his career. With six majors and over 25 tour events to his name Trevino was the confident kid with a quirky swing who charmed knowledgeable audiences around the world.

Lee Trevino was born into a fragmenting family in Dallas in 1939. Before he was old enough to remember his father walked out, leaving his Mexican mother and grandfather responsible for his upbringing. Money was a perpetual problem and before he was 10 years old Trevino would skip school to work in cotton fields to supplement the meagre family income. His schooling had finished altogether by the age of 14 as the need for cash exceeded the importance of gaining a comprehensive education. He took a job at a local driving range and it was here that his unlikely association with the game began. As an energetic teenager he would play whenever possible, and without anyone to guide him towards a mechanically sound technique he developed his own unique style.

When he reached the age of 17 Trevino opted for a secure income with the US Marines and served for four years. He was able to play, albeit sporadically, through this period and when he finished his tour of duty found a job as an assistant professional at a small club on the Mexican-American border.

Throughout Trevino's formative years he would take on any player willing to accept a challenge, regularly betting money that he simply didn't have on the outcome of a match against an opponent he barely knew. He was forced to back his talent and developed a ruthless mental streak ally to his natural ability that made him almost impossible to defeat. To entice sceptical punters into lucrative wagers he would often play using a strange device fashioned from insulating tape and a Coke bottle. He gambled on his talent, inadvertently developing his game for the pressure of tournament golf.

In 1965 Trevino won the Texas State Open and the following year he qualified to play in the US Open.

BELOW
Trevino is all smiles after winning the Senior Legends of Golf Championship in 1996.

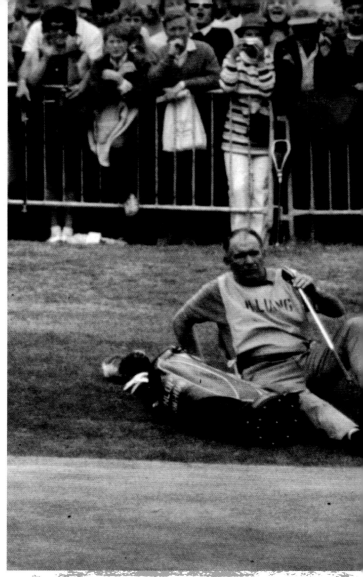

These achievements proved that a career playing golf could be lucrative, despite finishing way down the field in his first major appearance, Trevino clearly enjoyed his taste of golf at the highest level. In 1967 he returned to play in the same event at Baltusrol. Jack Nicklaus took the title but Trevino finished fifth and walked away with a cheque for $6,000. He loved the attention, valued the reward and took confidence from the knowledge that his game was fit for major golf.

"Supermex" won his first US Open in 1968 at Rochester in New York. Heading into the final round he trailed Bert Yancey by one stroke, but as Yancey struggled under the pressure so Trevino excelled, shooting 69 for the last 18 holes. Yancey's classic swing failed to stand up to Trevino's homemade version and the Mexican-American announced himself to the world in style, becoming the first winner of the US Open to complete all four rounds in the 60s. Furthermore, his ability to engage the crowd with amusing banter throughout the week endeared him to the public.

Trevino's second US Open victory in 1971, at Merion, pitted him against Jack Nicklaus in a tense play-off. Proving that he feared none of his more accomplished rivals, Trevino shot 69 to Nicklaus's 71. He soon added the British Open to his US crown, revealing that his game was strong enough to prevail on a variety of contrasting layouts.

Perhaps his most famous win though was the Open of 1972 at Muirfield. As the reigning champion he arrived on the East Lothian coast among the favourites to win. After three rounds the diminutive Mexican was closely pursued by Jack Nicklaus and Tony Jacklin.

When asked about how he would respond to the unique pressure of the situation Trevino famously told his interviewer, "try playing a hustler for $50 when you've only got $10 in your hip pocket. That's pressure." He proceeded to shoot a closing round 71 that included a chip in on the 17th to steal the momentum away from his English challenger.

Lee Trevino's career at the top level spanned three decades – his final major victory coming at the USPGA of 1984. His lively banter and ungainly swing contradicted the clinical strategy that made him such a consistent competitor and he played with a desperate desire to succeed that was always hidden beneath a disarming smile. Trevino's considerable achievements were a triumph of sheer natural talent emerging through an under-privileged background to scale the heights of the golfing world.

HARRY**VARDON**

Born in Jersey in 1870, Harry Vardon was the most successful member of "The Great Triumvirate". While James Braid and JH Taylor both won the Open five times, Vardon went one better and his record six remains unequalled today. He was also a truly international competitor, travelling three times to America to play in, and win, countless exhibition and challenge matches as well as the US Open. These remarkable achievements seem even more spectacular when you consider that Vardon suffered a debilitating illness for much of his adult life.

Unlike many of the great champions of the time, Vardon was certainly not destined to become a professional golfer. In fact it was not until 1877 that Jersey had a golf course, a project undertaken by a band of English visitors who designed a few holes near the Vardon family home. His father was a gardener and Harry himself had an array of different jobs through his early years – he worked on a dairy farm, assisted a doctor and served as a member of staff to a wealthy local Mayor. Indeed, it was Mayor Spofford of Beauview who encouraged Vardon's interest in the game, doubtless providing him with balls and clubs with which to play. Vardon left Jersey to take up the post as assistant professional at St. Annes in Lancashire and later moved to Studley Park where he was employed as both the professional and the greenkeeper.

Harry Vardon's early involvement in the game was purely as a means to make money, he did not compete very often and his brother Tom was regarded as the better player. But by 1894, Vardon's own game had reached a level that enabled him to compete in the Open at Sandwich. His creditable tie for fifth offered a glimpse of his talent.

In 1896 the Open was held at Muirfield and JH Taylor was looking to emulate Young Tom Morris's achievement of winning the Open three years in a row. Earlier in the season Taylor and Vardon had gone head-to-head in a challenge match and Vardon emerged victorious, winning comprehensively by 8&6. So despite leading Vardon by six shots at the half way stage, Taylor knew what his talented opponent was capable of. Vardon slowly chipped away at Taylor's lead and after 72 holes the two were level. Vardon won the ensuing 36-hole play-off convincingly by four shots. He was a worthy champion.

Having made this breakthrough, Vardon's self-confidence grew and he proceeded to win the Open twice more before the turn of the century. By this time

Born: Grouville, Jersey May 9, 1870
Died: March 20, 1937
Turned professional: 1890
Open: Winner in 1896, 1898, 1899, 1903, 1911, 1914
US Open: Winner in 1900

Harry Vardon had also played a crucial role in the increasing popularity of the game in the US. In 1913 he returned to America to compete in the now legendary US Open at Brookline, near Boston. At the half way stage Vardon held a healthy two shot lead over fellow Jersey islander Ted Ray and was four ahead of the amateur, Francis Ouimet. Completing the last seven holes in an awesome 26 shots, Ouimet managed to force a play-off with his two revered opponents. His one over par score of 72 for the 18 holes that ensued was five better than Vardon and six better than Ray. Despite losing this epic contest, Vardon had played his part in a dramatic passage of play that has since gone down in golfing folklore, capturing the imagination of the American people.

LEFT
Vardon chips from the rough, 1924.

BELOW
Vardon at the Open in 1920.

he was an established star at the top of his game, ready to take on new challenges.

In 1900, he crossed the Atlantic to embark on an extensive tour of the States that took him from New England to Florida, the highlight of which was the US Open in Chicago. He proved that the standard of British golf was high by taking the title by a staggering nine stroke margin. But despite this glorious achievement, Vardon's trip to the US was a bittersweet experience. He returned to the UK exhausted, physically weakened and from this time to his death in 1937 serious health problems including tuberculosis, meant that he frequently required hospital treatment. After winning the 1903 Open at Prestwick, where serious physical fatigue almost put a premature end to his challenge, he was admitted to a local sanatorium.

Vardon's next major victory came again in the Open Championship, eight years later. His final Open triumph in 1914 marked an end to the dominance of "The Great Triumvirate". Between them Vardon, Taylor and Braid had won the event 16 times in 20 years, their fierce rivalry and great skill had gone a long way to increase public interest in the sport.

Harry Vardon was a student of the game, he developed his own theory about how to hold and swing the club that broke tried and tested methods. He realised the importance of making his hands work together – although not the first to use it, he certainly popularised the overlapping grip that has since been dubbed 'The Vardon Grip'. His swing was fluid and more upright than his contemporaries with an aesthetic beauty that was fresh and far more reminiscent of what we see today.

TOM
WATSON

Born: Kansas City, Missouri, USA September 4, 1949

Turned professional: 1971

Masters: Winner in 1977, 1981

US Open: Winner in 1982

Open: Winner in 1975, 1977, 1980, 1982, 1983

USPGA: Tied 2nd in 1978

Ryder Cup record: Member of 4 US teams
(1977, 1981, 1983, 1989). Played 15, Won 10, Lost 4,
Halved 1. Captain in 1993

With a dynamic swing and aggressive strategy Tom Watson captivated audiences all around the world, emerging through a golden period in the game's history with eight majors to his name. His powerful yet compact swing was tailor made for the links and his achievements in our Open Championship are a monument to his masterful manipulation of the golf ball.

Despite not having a legacy of golf within the family Tom Watson's route into the professional ranks was fairly smooth. His father was a successful insurance broker and the Watson family enjoyed a comfortable living in Kansas City, Missouri. This enabled him to play golf at the nearby Prairie Dunes Country Club, where he developed an early infatuation with the game. After completing high school he enrolled at Stanford University to study psychology, marrying his academic and golfing education with success. By the age of 21, and with a handful of amateur titles under his belt, he then embarked on a career as a touring professional.

Tom Watson emerged through a successful American university system that continues to deliver high quality golfers to the Tour. However, his first few seasons were tough as he pitted his game against far more experienced players. Evidence of his immaturity at the highest level was seen at the US Open of 1974 when he entered the final round one shot ahead of Hale Irwin. The pressure of the situation and the severity of the challenge at Winged Foot proved too much for the 25-year-old and he shot a final round 79. Under the glare of an expectant American

public his game had fallen to pieces and Watson quickly developed a reputation as a choker.

He underlined his obvious talent however by winning the Western Open later that year and this first US Tour victory was the springboard for his emphatic arrival to the major winners' circle in 1975. The venue was Carnoustie on Scotland's east coast – a notoriously difficult layout – and Watson was making his Open debut. He was far better equipped to handle the pressure of the closing stages than the previous year and emerged to win a tight play-off against Australian Jack Newton by a single shot. Watson had triumphed at the Open on his first attempt, without even completing a full practice round, and it was clear that his game was suited to the links.

Two years later he won his first Green Jacket, narrowly defeating Jack Nicklaus by two shots. Their fierce but friendly rivalry was to be the star attraction when battle re-commenced that summer at Turnberry for

BELOW
Watson in the Buick Invitational, 1992 tournament.

the Open where a rare heatwave had parched the course. The hard, fast fairways and equally slick greens made for a low scoring Championship and in a barrage of birdies Watson and Nicklaus rose to the head of the field. Entering the final round the pair were tied after both had shot rounds of 68, 70 and 65. They sustained the birdie rush through the final afternoon, accelerating away from the field. Standing all square on the par 5 17th tee, Watson followed a long drive with a precise second into the heart of the green and two putted for a birdie. Nicklaus, however, came up short in two, chipped and two putted for a par. With a slender one-shot lead Watson split the final fairway with a supremely struck 1-iron. Nicklaus was forced to attack at all costs and pushed his drive, narrowly avoiding a bush to the right of the fairway. From there Nicklaus found the green, albeit 30ft from the hole, and the pressure was back on Watson who responded with a sparkling 7-iron to 25ins. In one last twist Nicklaus holed his 30 footer, forcing Watson to make his short putt for the title. He duly did so and the 'duel in the sun', as it became known, remains one of the greatest final round battles of all time.

Watson won the Open again in 1980 at Muirfield, before claiming his only US Open victory in 1982. The venue was Pebble Beach and once again it was Jack Nicklaus applying the pressure. The two were tied on the par-3 17th but Watson was in dire straits having pulled his tee shot into deep rough to the left of the green. Remarkably, he holed his recovery shot and again defeated Nicklaus by a single stroke.

Back-to-back victories in 1982 and 1983 made it five Open crowns for Watson, equalling the achievements of JH Taylor and James Braid, and in 1984 he came within touching distance of Harry Vardon's super six. But a wayward approach to the St. Andrews road hole in the final round, and an inspired performance by a 27-year-old Seve Ballesteros, conspired against Watson and Vardon's record remained in tact.

Tom Watson's achievements seem even more remarkable when you consider the calibre of the players he consistently beat. From Trevino and Nicklaus to Ballesteros and Faldo, Watson proved that aggressive, exciting golf could be a successful formula. He was a modern day master of the links who still holds a special place in the hearts of British golf fans.

Legends of **GOLF**

KATHY**WHITWORTH**

It's quite extraordinary that Kathy Whitworth only managed to capture six major Ladies Professional Golf Association titles during her long career, for her overall tournament-winning record is unrivalled.

For evidence of Kathy's importance to the history of golf, feast your eyes on this statistic: she won 88 times on the LPGA tour, and that's more than any other player,

male or female, has ever won on any tour. Her first LPGA victory came at the Kelly Girl Open in 1962, and her last came 23 long years later, at the 1985 United Virginia Bank Classic. For a long time, Kathy Whitworth simply WAS women's golf.

The records and impressive stats go on and on… Kathy, for example, was the LPGA Tour's leading money winner on eight occasions between 1965 and 1973, missing out only once, in 1969. She was the LPGA's Player of the Year no fewer than seven times, and picked up the Vare Trophy – awarded annually to the LPGA golfer with the lowest scoring average in the preceding year – seven times between 1965 and 1972. That's another LPGA record, and Kathy was only prevented from making it eight Vare Trophies by Carol Mann's performance in 1968.

She was a great woman for holes in one, and her total of 11 during her LPGA career is another record for the association. And it should come as no great surprise to learn that Kathy was the first LPGA player to exceed $1 million in career earnings. She passed that milestone when she finished third in the 1981 US Women's Open.

One further fact illustrates her grip on the game superbly: she won at least one tournament every year between 1962 and 1978, setting yet another LPGA record in the process.

What made Kathy Whitworth so good? She worked hard, she was blessed with splendid technique, being renowned for her driving and putting excellence, and her powers of concentration were legendary. And yet, her career in professional golf started so slowly that at one point, thoroughly dispirited, she considered giving it all up.

Kathy, born in Texas but raised in New Mexico, first picked up a golf club at the age of 15, and learned quickly. She was good enough by 1957 to win the New Mexico State Amateur tournament, a feat she repeated the following year, and it seemed a natural progression when she joined the professional ranks in December 1958. But success was a long time – four years, to be exact – in coming and it was only a visit to the revered instructor Harvey Penick that convinced her she had the ability to make it big in the pro game. Then came that

Born: Monahans, Texas, USA September 27, 1939

Turned professional: 1958

LPGA Championship: Winner in 1967, 1971, 1975

US Women's Open: 2nd in 1971, 3rd in 1969 and 1981

Titleholders Championship: Winner in 1965, 1966

Western Open: Winner in 1967

LEFT
Kathy Whitworth pictured with the Solheim Cup after captaining the USA in 1990.

first tournament win, in 1962, and Kathy's career took off in a miraculous fashion.

At this point, it's worth returning to the facts and figures to illustrate her impact on women's golf in the 1960s. In 1965, just three years after that initial victory in the Kelly Girl Open, she won no fewer than eight tournaments. She followed that up with nine wins in 1966, eight again in 1967 and 10 in 1968.

Along the way, Kathy signed for a seven-under par 62 in the third round of the 1968 Holiday Inn Classic, on her way to winning the tournament. It equalled Mickey Wright's score in the 1964 Tall City Open as the lowest third round in the history of the LPGA, and for a long time, until the feat was equalled by Juli Inkster in 2003, it was also the lowest final round by a winner in the association's history.

Kathy was, of course, picking up major titles as her career progressed, but she was never to add the US Women's Open to her prize list; the closest she ever came was a second place in 1971. And as the 1970s wore on,

her game began to suffer from the intensity of playing at the top year after year. But there were still targets to aim for, including the $1 million earnings total and the record for the total number of tournament wins, held jointly by Sam Snead and Mickey Wright with 82.

It was only a matter of time, and Kathy registered win number 83 with a 40-foot putt at the final hole of the 1983 Kemper Open. She won three times in each of the following two years to post that figure of 88 tournament victories.

Kathy Whitworth's record-breaking contribution to golf was recognised in her vice-presidency and presidency of the LPGA, and when she captained the USA team in the first two Solheim Cups, in 1990 and 1992.

Will her tournament-win record ever be bettered? Only Annika Sorenstam, of the current crop of women golfers, can dream of coming close, and Tiger Woods in the men's game has a chance if he continues his winning ways. Time will tell.

TIGER
WOODS

Born: Cypress, California, USA December 30, 1975
Turned professional: 1996
Masters: Winner in 1997, 2001, 2002, 2005
US Open: Winner in 2000, 2002
Open: Winner in 2000, 2005, 2006
USPGA: Winner in 1999, 2000, 2006
Ryder Cup record: Member of 5 US teams
(1997, 1999, 2002, 2004, 2006). Played 25, Won 10, Lost 13,
Halved 2

For Tiger Woods to be universally recognised as the greatest golfer to have lived he will have to surpass Jack Nicklaus's record of 18 major victories. This remains the only milestone of any serious significance untouched by a man whose phenomenal natural talent, physical might and psychological strength have swept his peers mercilessly aside. His athletic yet smooth style coupled with his ruthless and successful pursuit of glory have made him a multi-million dollar commercial asset like no golfer before him. His presence in the field single-handedly raises the profile of any event, guaranteeing international audiences and vast galleries. The world now waits with bated breath to see just how far Tiger Woods can go.

Looking closely at his upbringing, it would appear that Tiger Woods was destined to become a top-flight golfer. Even as early as six months old, he would mimic his father's golf swing and by the age of three he had a score of 48 for nine holes and a television appearance in which he putted alongside Bob Hope under his belt.

The crucial influence in Tiger's early attraction to the game was undoubtedly his father. Earl Woods had served as a lieutenant colonel in the US Army and was quick to spot and nurture his son's talent. (Indeed, it was Earl who gave his son the nickname Tiger after a close military friend of the same title.) As a junior, Tiger's phenomenal talent was clear from the start. He became the youngest ever winner of the US Junior Championship, aged just 15 and the following year he was good enough to warrant a place in his first professional event, the Nissan Los Angeles Open. In 1994, he enrolled at

Stanford University, where his game developed under a structured coaching regime. Competing at University enabled Woods to pit his game against many of the world's best amateurs – he won 10 collegiate events and earned a place in the 1995 Walker Cup. After capturing his third consecutive US Amateur title in 1996 it was clear that having conquered the amateur world Tiger Woods was ready for life on Tour.

His decision to turn pro in August 1996 left just seven events to secure his playing privileges for the following year. Remarkably, he won twice and finished in the top 10 three times to propel himself to 25th place on the moneylist. In a career littered with glory, this remains one of his finest achievements.

Tiger's first major triumph came at the US Masters in 1997 but after the opening nine holes he appeared to have blown his chances with a disastrous four over par score of 40. From the 10th tee his form returned spectacularly – he shot 30 for the inward half and followed his opening round of 70 with scores of 66, 65 and 69. At 21, he became the youngest ever Masters

BELOW
Woods in action at the Players Championship Sawgrass, 2000.

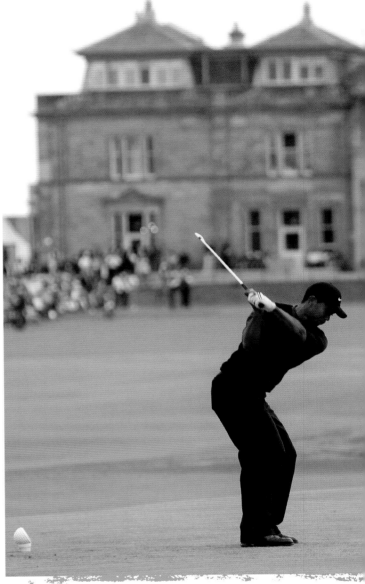

champion and his staggering 12-shot winning margin was a new record. It was a performance built on power and control, proving that Woods was a cut above the best players on the planet. He quickly added to this success and by mid-June 1997, the world had a new number one golfer. Still just 21, Tiger Woods became the youngest man to reach this milestone.

His finest season to date however was in 2000. The first of his three major victories arrived at Pebble Beach in the US Open. In wet and windy conditions, the field struggled to tame a course set up by the USGA to push the best players in the world to the limit. Woods laid on a masterclass that was virtually perfect in every department of the game. He finished the event on 12 with his coach, Butch Harmon, Woods decided to regulate his swing by himself. From the outside this looked a strange decision and his form duly dipped. Vijay Singh muscled in to take his world number one spot in September 2004 and Tiger lost his air of invincibility. As frustrating as it was for Woods, media criticism of his decision to part with Harmon was inevitable. Each week on Tour his technique was pulled apart by former players attempting to explain why Tiger was unable to tame his driver. At the start of 2004, Woods employed the services of swing-guru, Hank Haney and the adjustments the two made paid off as Tiger returned to his best by winning the 2005 Masters and Open and the 2006 Open and USPGA.

With 12 majors already to his name, it might seem strange to say it but Tiger Woods is entering a critical phase in his career. If he is to stand proudly as the finest golfer of all time he will need to march on relentlessly through his 30s. But regardless of whether he reaches Jack Nicklaus's record or not, it will be a journey that no true golf fan will want to miss.

LEFT
Woods on the final tee of the 2005 Open, in which he secured victory.

FAR LEFT
Tiger Woods in the Masters play-off 2005, celebrates sinking a putt on his way to the title.

BELOW
Woods with the 1999 USPGA trophy.

under par – no other player managed to break into red figures. His 15-stroke winning margin smashed the previous record of 13 set by Old Tom Morris, 138 years earlier. Many believe this to be the finest strokeplay performance in the history of the sport.

Woods maintained this level of performance to capture the two remaining majors in 2000 and become the youngest player to win each of the big four. Then when he took the 2001 Masters, he became the only golfer ever to hold all four majors simultaneously.

During this period of supremacy few would have questioned that they were watching the most talented golfer of all time. But through 2003 and 2004 Tiger failed to win a single major. Having parted company

IAN**WOOSNAM**

He may stand only 5ft 4ins in his stockinged feet, but he packs a hell of a punch when he steps up to whack the ball off the tee. And his impact on world golf has been out of all proportion to his physical size.

The powerhouse and supremely talented golfer that is Ian Woosnam has won 44 tournaments all over the world, was world number one for a while and helped Europe's Ryder Cup resurgence through the 1980s and 1990s. The highlights of this marvellous career, though, have been his victory at the 1991 Masters and his inspired captaincy of the 2006 European Ryder Cup team that annihilated the Americans at the K Club in Ireland.

Woosnam started playing with a shortened set of clubs when he was just seven. Fifteen of the holes at the Llanymynech Golf Club, where he first started to learn his craft, are in Wales while the other three are over the border in England, but there's no room for doubt as to his national loyalties: Woosie is a Welshman through and through who has represented his country many times.

The early promise of a rewarding career in golf was there from an early age, but after turning pro in 1976 Woosie struggled for what must have seemed like an eternity. It took him three attempts to qualify for the European tour and, even after he did so, times were hard. The young golfer earned just £6,000 in his first five years on the tour, and the story is often told of how he travelled around Europe in a camper van, living on baked beans. This restricted diet did nothing to limit his physical prowess, however. Years of working on his father's farm had given the young Woosnam a strength that allowed him to out-hit much more physically imposing golfers.

And happier days were just around the corner. Woosie won his first tournament – the Ebel Swiss Open – in 1982, followed it up with the 1983 Silk Cut Masters and was on his way to glory.

By 1987, he was on top of the world – literally. He became the first player to win £1 million in prize money in a single year, and he chalked up a staggering eight tournament victories, including the Suntory World Match Play and the Hong Kong Open, in doing so. Even greater things were to follow.

Woosnam's winning ways continued throughout the late 80s and early 90s, and they reached their zenith in 1991. At the start of the year, he'd set himself three targets: winning in the US, winning a major and topping the world rankings. He achieved all three.

Born: Oswestry, Shropshire, England
March 2, 1958

Turned professional: 1976

Masters: Winner in 1991

US Open: Tied 2nd in 1989

Open: Tied 3rd in 1986, 2001

Ryder Cup record: Member of 8 European teams (1983, 1985, 1987, 1989, 1991, 1993, 1995, 1997). Played 31, Won 14, List 12, Halved 5. Captain in 2006

Legends of **GOLF**

If that was a low point of his career, there have been many high points, and the Ryder Cup has provided more than a few. What a team player Woosie proved, winning 14 of the 23 fourballs and foursomes he played – although his record in the singles was much less impressive.

His dedication to the European cause was rewarded with the captaincy of the team for the 2006 event. And he duly inspired his men to an astonishing repeat of the 18.5 – 9.5 scoreline of the 2004 match. It was a fitting climax to a wonderful Ryder Cup career.

If 1991 was Woosie's year, the Masters was his tournament of the year. In a tense finish at Augusta, he saw off the challenges of Jose Maria Olazabal and Tom Watson, parring the final hole with an eight-foot putt while his rivals faltered. It was enough to earn him the famed green jacket and top spot in the world rankings – where he stayed for the following 51 weeks, a record at the time.

The next few years saw Woosnam picking up more tournament wins on the European Tour, with four victories in 1996 proving the highlight. And although he was never to return to the heights of that glorious year of 1991, it was not until 2001 that he won his final trophy, for the Cisco World Match Play. That year also saw an extraordinary near miss at the Open Championship at Royal Lytham.

By then aged 43, Woosnam suffered the indignity of a two-stroke penalty for having too many clubs in his bag – 15 instead of the permitted 14 – at a crucial moment in the final round. He had just birdied the first to share the lead when caddie Miles Byrne's error was discovered, and the shock and the penalty were enough to ensure Woosie finished three shots behind winner David Duval. "It took me a few holes to recover and I didn't really get it out of my head all the way round," said the rueful Woosnam.

MICKEY**WRIGHT**

Was Mickey Wright the best woman golfer ever to grace the Ladies Professional Golf Association, or even the best in the game's history? There are those who believe so, and they have ample ammunition to back up their claim.

Mickey (born Mary Kathryn) Wright won the stunning total of 82 events on the LPGA Tour, and only Kathy Whitworth won more. As for the major championships, Mickey walked away with 13 victories, a total only topped by Patty Berg. She won 12 majors between 1958 and 1966 and she holds the unique distinction of being the only LPGA player to hold all four major titles at the same time.

Born: San Diego, California, USA
February 14, 1935

Turned professional: 1955

US Women's Open: Winner in 1958, 1959, 1961, 1964, 2nd in 1968, 3rd in 1966, tied 3rd in 1971

Titleholders Championship: Winner in 1961, 1962

LPGA Championship: Winner in 1958, 1960, 1961, 1963, 2nd in 1964, 1966

Western Open: Winner in 1962, 1963, 1966

And all this was achieved in an incredibly short space of time. There were only 14 years between Mickey's first LPGA tournament win – the Jacksonville Open in 1956 – and her retirement from regular play due to foot troubles, a dislike of flying and the sheer pressure of being the player everyone wanted to watch.

There are more arguments behind the stats to support the theory that blue-eyed blonde Mickey was the greatest. You have only to listen to her fellow golfers' eulogies to realise that she was something very special indeed.

Betsy Rawls, Ben Hogan, Beth Daniel and Byron Nelson were among those who insisted that Mickey's swing was the best they ever saw. Rawls went further, writing in Golf Digest: "As people watched Mickey play golf … what they saw was a nearly perfect golf swing, a display of power not seen since Babe Zaharias, and golf shots unlike any that had been produced by women golfers up until then."

Rawls also noted Mickey's striving to be perfect, to be the best, and the pressure she put herself under to achieve that goal. "Miss-hit shots that ended up close to the hole did not give Mickey much satisfaction," she wrote.

The drive for perfection was evident in Mickey from an early age. She swung her first golf club when she was 11 and was soon winning tournaments including the 1954 World Amateur. A brief sojourn at Stanford University, studying psychology, ended in 1955 when she joined the LPGA Tour.

By the end of 1957 – a year in which she won three tournaments – she had made a massive impact on the Tour. She followed with three wins in each of the following years, but she was really only warming up.

There were five victories in 1960, and then Mickey really got going, chalking up 10 or more tournament wins every year until 1964. It's worth pointing out here that she hoisted at least one LPGA Tour trophy aloft every year between 1956 and 1969, a winning run that has only been bettered by Kathy Whitworth, and that she posted 13 victories alone in 1963.

Mickey was the LPGA Tour money leader on four occasions in the early 60s; won the Vare Trophy for the best scoring average every year from 1960 to 1965; and

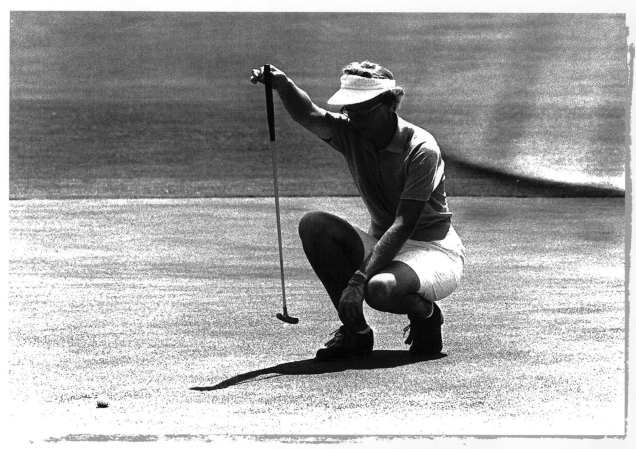

was named Woman Athlete of the Year for 1963-64 by the Associated Press.

And all this time, the major championships were piling up. Mickey won the US Women's Open and the LPGA Championship four times each, the Western Open three times and the Titleholders twice. There is confirmation of another impressive statistic coming up here: by winning the US Women's Open and the LPGA Championship in 1961 and carrying on into 1962 by claiming the Titleholders Championship and the Western Open, she became the only LPGA player in history to hold all four major titles simultaneously. That record has never been beaten.

Did all those victories make Mickey Wright a rich woman? Well, she was certainly comfortable financially, but it's extraordinary to think that the $30,000 she collected for finishing second in the Sprint Senior Challenge of 1994 was the largest cheque of her career.

By that time, of course, Mickey was turning out only very occasionally, but she'd still got the bug.

So what was it that about her game, apart from that classic swing and her drive for perfection, that brought her so much success? It has to be said that Mickey was never the world's greatest putter, but she worked hard at improving her performance on the green, and at perfecting other elements of her short game. Perhaps the greatest secret of her success was an extraordinary ability to concentrate, to block out all extraneous influences and focus on the job in hand.

Mickey was only 34 when she decided she could no longer continue at the high level she had reached, and called an end to her full-time golf career. She had dedicated her life to being the best, and could not contemplate a time when she could not guarantee remaining at that standard. The world lost one of its all-time greats.

BABE**ZAHARIAS**

Babe Zaharias would win her place in any book about golf legends very comfortably. She could also have staked justifiable claims for inclusion in books about legends of basketball, baseball, track and field athletics, swimming, diving, tennis… you name a sport and Babe probably excelled at it.

She was just that kind of woman. She was good at anything she tried – and she tried most sports during a life that was cut tragically short. In fact, some folk say she was the greatest all-round athlete, of either gender, there has ever been. It's certainly hard to think of anyone better qualified for that title.

Babe was born Mildred Didriksen (she later changed the spelling to Didrikson), the daughter of Norwegian immigrant parents to the USA, and it wasn't long before she was making an indelible mark on the world of sport. It's said that she was nicknamed Babe after baseball legend Babe Ruth, after hitting five home runs in one game, and such was her prowess on the basketball court that a Dallas company offered her employment as a secretary while she was still at high school – as long as she played for the company team.

But it was in another sporting field altogether that Babe really imprinted herself on the world's consciousness. She excelled at track and field athletics, and was soon setting world records in the 80m hurdles, the high jump and the javelin. Then came the 1932 Olympic Games in Los Angeles, and a turning point in Babe's sporting career.

As expected, she won gold medals in the hurdles and javelin, and would probably have won the high jump too, if she hadn't been disqualified, rather harshly. But it was during the Olympics that the 21-year-old Babe was introduced to the game of golf by sports writer Grantland Rice. In her first round, we're told by Rice, she shot a 91 and pumped out 250-yard drives. This woman was a natural at everything she tried.

Lessons followed, and it wasn't long before Babe's golf career was under way. She won the second event she ever took part in – the 1935 Texas Women's Invitational – but was subsequently judged to be a professional by the US Golf Association because of the money she'd earned in other sports.

Nothing daunted, Babe set out on the exhibition and pro-am golf circuit, and even competed in the Los Angeles Open, a men's PGA tournament, in 1938. There she found herself playing with a certain George

Born: Port Arthur, Texas, USA June 26, 1911
Died: September 27, 1956
Turned professional: 1938
US Women's Open: Winner in 1948, 1950, 1954
Titleholders Championship: Winner in 1947, 1950, 1952
Western Open: Winner in 1940, 1944, 1945, 1950

Legends of **GOLF**

time: the US Women's Open, the Titleholders Championship and the Western Open.

In all, Babe recorded 10 wins in majors and 41 victories in professional tournaments during her career. It should be noted that five of those 41 wins came while she was an amateur.

The winning was not to continue for ever. The golf world held its breath when news came through in 1953 that Babe was suffering from cancer of the colon. But she didn't let a little thing like that, or the surgery she underwent, stop her for long. Just months after the surgery, Babe was winning the US Women's Open again.

The cancer was not to be denied, however. It returned to claim Babe Zaharias' life in 1956 – but not before she had triumphed in the Tampa Open and the Peach Blossom Classic in 1955.

Golf – and a lot of other sports – had lost one hell of a woman.

LEFT
Zaharias chips from a bunker, 1946.

BELOW
Babe Zaharias on the putting green in the 1940s.

Zaharias, a professional wrestler and sports promoter, and the pair of them got together, in both marital and management terms.

Babe Zaharias was, naturally, as good at golf as she was at all the other sports she tried. Perhaps she wasn't the most elegant of golfers, but she had a natural athlete's ability to get the most out her physique. Weighing not much more than 10st 5lb, she still clubbed out those 250-yard drives, and when she was asked how she did it, she famously replied: "I just loosen my girdle and take a whack at it."

The USGA reinstated Babe's amateur status in 1943, and she proceeded to dominate the women's game. Among her tournament victories were the US Women's Amateur in 1946 and the British Women's Amateur in 1947, and at one point she won an astonishing 16 consecutive events.

So it was, inevitably, that she returned to the professional ranks in 1947, and her impact on the pro game was massive. She was one of the 13 founders of the Ladies Professional Golfers Association in 1950, which happened to be her greatest golf year ever. Having already won four major championships while she was an amateur, and added two more in the intervening years, Babe completed the grand slam in 1950 by carrying off all three of the LPGA's three majors of the

THE PICTURES IN THIS BOOK WERE PROVIDED COURTESY OF THE FOLLOWING:

GETTY**IMAGES**
101 Bayham Street, London NW1 0AG

EMPICS
www.empics.com

PHIL**SHELDON**GOLF**PICTURE**LIBRARY
40 Manor Way, Barnet, Hertfordshire EN5 2JQ

Concept and Art Direction:
VANESSA **and** KEVIN**GARDNER**

Creative and Artwork: KEVIN**GARDNER**

Image research: ELLIE**CHARLESTON**

PUBLISHED BY GREEN UMBRELLA PUBLISHING

Publishers:
JULES**GAMMOND and** VANESSA**GARDNER**

Written by: NEIL**TAPPIN and** PATRICK**MORGAN**